NEW DIRECTIONS FOR EVALUATION
A PUBLICATION OF THE AMERICAN EVALUATION

The Mainstreaming of Evaluation

J. Jackson Barnette
University of Iowa College of Public Health

James R. Sanders
Western Michigan University

EDITORS

Number 99, Fall 2003

JOSSEY-BASS
San Francisco

THE MAINSTREAMING OF EVALUATION
J. Jackson Barnette, James R. Sanders (eds.)
New Directions for Evaluation, no. 99
Jennifer C. Greene, Gary T. Henry, Coeditors-in-Chief

Microfilm copies of issues and articles are available in 16mm and 35mm, as well as microfiche in 105mm, through University Microfilms Inc., 300 North Zeeb Road, Ann Arbor, Michigan 48106-1346.

New Directions for Evaluation is indexed in Contents Pages in Education, Higher Education Abstracts, and Sociological Abstracts.

Print ISSN: 1097-6736; Online ISSN: 1534-875X

NEW DIRECTIONS FOR EVALUATION is part of The Jossey-Bass Education Series and is published quarterly by Wiley Subscription Services, Inc., a Wiley company, at Jossey-Bass, 989 Market Street, San Francisco, California 94103-1741.

SUBSCRIPTIONS cost $80.00 for U.S./Canada/Mexico; $104 international. For institutions, agencies, and libraries, $175 U.S.; $215 Canada; $249 international. Prices subject to change.

EDITORIAL CORRESPONDENCE should be addressed to the Editors-in-Chief, Jennifer C. Greene, Department of Educational Psychology, University of Illinois, 260E Education Building, 1310 South Sixth Street, Champaign, IL 61820, or Gary T. Henry, School of Policy Studies, Georgia State University, P.O. Box 4039, Atlanta, GA 30302-4039.

www.josseybass.com

NEW DIRECTIONS FOR EVALUATION

Sponsored by the American Evaluation Association

AMERICAN EVALUATION ASSOCIATION, 16 SCONTICUT ROAD #290, FAIRHAVEN, MA 02719.
WWW.EVAL.ORG

Editorial Policy and Procedures

New Directions for Evaluation, a quarterly sourcebook, is an official publication of the American Evaluation Association. The journal publishes empirical, methodological, and theoretical works on all aspects of evaluation. A reflective approach to evaluation is an essential strand to be woven through every volume. The editors encourage volumes that have one of three foci: (1) craft volumes that present approaches, methods, or techniques that can be applied in evaluation practice, such as the use of templates, case studies, or survey research; (2) professional issue volumes that present issues of import for the field of evaluation, such as utilization of evaluation or locus of evaluation capacity; (3) societal issue volumes that draw out the implications of intellectual, social, or cultural developments for the field of evaluation, such as the women's movement, communitarianism, or multiculturalism. A wide range of substantive domains is appropriate for *New Directions for Evaluation;* however, the domains must be of interest to a large audience within the field of evaluation. We encourage a diversity of perspectives and experiences within each volume, as well as creative bridges between evaluation and other sectors of our collective lives.

The editors do not consider or publish unsolicited single manuscripts. Each issue of the journal is devoted to a single topic, with contributions solicited, organized, reviewed, and edited by a guest editor. Issues may take any of several forms, such as a series of related chapters, a debate, or a long article followed by brief critical commentaries. In all cases, the proposals must follow a specific format, which can be obtained from the editor-in-chief. These proposals are sent to members of the editorial board and to relevant substantive experts for peer review. The process may result in acceptance, a recommendation to revise and resubmit, or rejection. However, the editors are committed to working constructively with potential guest editors to help them develop acceptable proposals.

Jennifer C. Greene, Coeditor-in-Chief
Department of Educational Psychology
University of Illinois
260E Education Building
1310 South Sixth Street
Champaign, IL 61820
e-mail: jcgreene@uiuc.edu

Gary T. Henry, Coeditor-in-Chief
School of Policy Studies
Georgia State University
P.O. Box 4039
Atlanta, GA 30302-4039
e-mail: gthenry@gsu.edu

CONTENTS

EDITORS' NOTES

The theme for the 2001 annual meeting of the American Evaluation Association (AEA) was mainstreaming evaluation. The primary question surrounding presentations on this theme was, How can—and should—evaluation be mainstreamed in organizations? There was never any debate about whether evaluation was widely mainstreamed in 2001. It was not.

Three chapters in this issue won the Presidential Prize for contributions to the conference theme (Wandersman and others, Grudens-Schuck, and Duignan). The other three chapters were commissioned to complement the prize-winning contributions (Sanders, Barnette and Wallis, and Williams and Hawkes).

The Sanders chapter provides a definition of the concept of mainstreaming evaluation, a case example, reasons given for not mainstreaming evaluation, and recommendations for the future. This chapter and Sanders's presidential address (Sanders, 2002) provide a foundation for the chapters that follow.

Duignan describes some approaches to mainstreaming evaluation that appear to be successful in New Zealand, particularly in human services programs that serve both European and Maori populations. Grudens-Schuck, an educational anthropologist, discusses her observations about the role of authors in mainstreaming in the context of an evaluation in Indonesia. She found that although the evaluation was described as participatory, in fact, it was not. She wrestles with the meaning of participatory evaluation and questions the usual assertion that a particular type of evaluation is appropriate in every context. Wandersman and colleagues offer a case history of their experience in helping implement a program accountability system within a state educational initiative. This chapter should be of particular interest to evaluators and policymakers who are looking for concrete approaches to integrating evaluative activities into a large program.

Barnette and Wallis propose ideas for broadening graduate training in evaluation research methods in order to infuse the practice with professionals who are equipped to promote mainstreaming. They focus on classroom and practical experiences for students and postgraduates to help them understand evaluation as a three-dimensional activity that, in the best of situations, is ingrained in program structure rather than an afterthought.

We express our sincere thanks to Gary Henry, coeditor-in-chief of *New Directions for Evaluation*. His encouragement and advice were instrumental in the completion of this issue. We also express our sincere thanks to Anne Baber Wallis, who was very helpful in editing the chapter drafts, and LaRae Rudin for her preparation of the chapters for submission.

Students should emerge from their graduate training prepared to practice evaluation in a participatory manner and with a good understanding about how evaluation research contributes to academic and public discourse about programmatic interventions and the communities served.

Williams and Hawkes were asked to attend Presidential Strand sessions at the 2001 conference. They have summarized and organized the content of these sessions into a single chapter that includes a wide range of viewpoints and ideas about mainstreaming.

In total, the chapters in this issue introduce an important concept: developing an evaluation culture at all levels of organizations across the fields of business, education, government, health and human services, and nonprofit agencies. The authors analyze the concept and provide a compilation of the many important issues that surround it.

We hope that this issue of *New Directions in Evaluation* will prove to be provocative and motivational to readers. It will be interesting to revisit the concept of mainstreaming evaluation a decade from now to see whether the same concerns about evaluation remain or whether new directions have indeed been taken.

J. Jackson Barnette
James R. Sanders
Editors

J. JACKSON BARNETTE is associate professor of community and behavioral health and director of the Center for Public Health Program Evaluation at the University of Iowa College of Public Health. He also serves as associate dean for education and student affairs and director of the master's in public health program in the College of Public Health. He served as chair of the AEA Presidential Strand on Mainstreaming in 2001.

JAMES R. SANDERS is professor emeritus of educational studies at Western Michigan University. He served as associate director of the Evaluation Center at WMU from 1975 until his retirement in 2001, chaired the Joint Committee on Standards for Educational Evaluation from 1988 until 1998, and was president of the AEA in 2001.

1

The concept of mainstreaming evaluation is defined, and the question of why mainstreaming is not more prevalent is addressed. A case of mainstreaming evaluation in a community hospice is presented, along with recommendations for moving organizations toward mainstreaming evaluation. This chapter and Sanders's AEA presidential address (2002) provide a foundation for the discussion of mainstreaming evaluation.

Mainstreaming Evaluation

James R. Sanders

If evaluation is seen as a means to the ends of successfully reaching goals, of improving services and products, of navigating change that responds to an ever-changing environment, of moving ever closer to excellence, why is it still in the margins of organizations? Why is it not a required course of study in the preparation of educational, business, public, or nonprofit administrators or in the training of leaders in these fields? These questions have prompted me to explore the reasons for the limited visibility that evaluation has in practice and in the preparation for administration and leadership. They have also started me thinking about paths to moving evaluation out of the margins and into the mainstream of organizational life.

Elsewhere (Sanders, 2002), I have defined *mainstreaming* as the process of making evaluation an integral part of an organization's everyday operations. Mainstreaming evaluation would make it part of the organization's work ethic, its culture, and job responsibilities at all levels. I have not attempted to define appropriate evaluation approaches, methods, designs, or tasks for organizations, nor would I want to. These decisions are situational and should be the responsibility of those who work within the organization, advise its workers, and oversee its operations and policies.

Why Isn't Evaluation Mainstreamed?

In my interviews with leaders in business, government, education, and nonprofit organizations, I have found a pattern of responses that shed light on this question. These leaders say that evaluation is not mainstreamed because

- We aren't aware of its benefits. Can you point to organizations like ours that are successful because of their evaluation practices?

- Evaluation can be costly, and we thrive on efficiency. Can you give us cost-benefit data from organizations like ours that have invested in evaluation?
- There aren't enough trained evaluation leaders to go around. Where can we find evaluators who can make evaluation work for us?
- Most evaluations that have been imposed on us have had little or no effect on our work. If anything, they have negatively affected us. Evaluation has distracted us from the real work that we should be doing. Our experience with evaluation has been mostly negative.

Let us consider each of these reasons for not mainstreaming evaluation.

We Aren't Aware of Benefits. First, I agree that there are too few published case studies of evaluation use in different fields. How can we learn and teach about the benefits of evaluation in business, education, public administration, and nonprofits without concrete examples? The Drucker Foundation gives awards for excellence in the management of human service organizations, but it does not make their evaluation practices visible. An awards program for exemplary evaluation practices in different fields is needed to compile and distribute cases of mainstreaming evaluation.

For example, I describe one case here of a community organization that has mainstreamed evaluation. There are lessons to be learned from just this one case. The director of the organization (a hospice) has attached evaluation procedures to each activity the agency undertakes so the agencies can see how well they are doing. These procedures include satisfaction surveys, focus groups, case analyses (strengths and weaknesses), statistical data collection, benchmarking, quality circles or problem-solving groups, chart reviews, periodic monitoring, and staff recognition for suggestions that will improve the effectiveness of the organization (one example: coffee mugs that say "Make Us Great"). In addition, part of the orientation of each new staff member includes a message that all staff members are responsible for continuously improving their own and the organization's performance. The agency supports this goal through staff development opportunities. Also a total quality improvement coordinator is responsible for overseeing all evaluation activities and for generating all evaluation reports. An evaluation advisory committee is the oversight group that makes recommendations based on the results of evaluation. It is composed of members of the staff, community, and board of directors. The director of this organization supports evaluation by allocating resources for it and by participating in most evaluation activities. This organization is strong financially and in its productivity. It is viewed as one of the most effective human service agencies in the community.

Evaluation Can Be Costly. Again, we lack enough cases to be able to respond to the cost-benefit question across business, education, public administration, and nonprofit organizations. The director of the hospice organization I described responds that the cost of evaluation is part of the cost of doing business. Underlying this response is a belief that evaluation is simply good management. Elsewhere, Scriven (1991) provides arguments on the costs of *not* mainstreaming evaluation. These arguments are reproduced in Sanders (2002).

There Aren't Enough Leaders. The lack of evaluation leadership for business, education, public administration, and nonprofit organizations reflects the dearth of formal preservice training in evaluation for administrators and leaders in these areas. Few universities provide even a course in evaluation in their colleges of business, arts and sciences, health and human services, and education. Inservice training in evaluation through such organizations as the AEA (www.eval.org) does little to reach leaders and administrators in business, education, government, and nonprofit organizations.

At best, organizational consultants are now being hired to plan and implement evaluation processes for organizations, but the number of qualified consultants is very limited, and their presence in the organization is temporary; long-term evaluation leadership is needed. In my judgment, university faculty who read this chapter must take the lead in preparing evaluators for leadership roles in organizations or in preparing leaders for evaluation roles in organizations.

Evaluations Have Little Effect. Evaluation mandates are often ill-conceived because they are planned and approved by individuals with little training or experience in evaluation and in the organizations that must carry out the mandates. Those who receive such ill-conceived evaluation mandates must be able to respond constructively with new proposals that will be useful, feasible, ethical, and accurate. Experience with evaluation should help guide this response. *The Program Evaluation Standards* (Joint Committee on Standards for Educational Evaluation, 1994) should also provide guidance. Asking for an outside expert review of evaluation requirements can also help to head off ill-conceived evaluation mandates. The argument I would use here is that poor evaluation can be worse than no evaluation at all for an organization. Evaluation should be beneficial and productive, or changes should be proposed. Blindly carrying out poorly conceived evaluation orders is simply not good practice. Poor mandates are not a good reason for avoiding beneficial, well-conceived evaluation practices, however. Members of the organization should argue for and do what they can and what they think is right when it comes to evaluation.

What Can We Do to Mainstream Evaluation?

I have suggested new directions for the future elsewhere (Sanders, 2002) and would like to refine those recommendations here. We need to do the following:

- *Identify and work with allies who recognize the value of building an evaluation culture.* Allies may include the Drucker Foundation, which could publish cases of organizations that have mainstreamed evaluation, and the AEA, which could begin an award and publicity program for business, education, government, and nonprofit organizations that have successfully mainstreamed evaluation. Universities (colleges of business, education, government, and human services), as well as associations serving leaders and administrators in the four fields, are important yet untapped allies for preparing organizational leaders with a vision of mainstreaming evaluation.

- *Compile and publish case histories of organizations that have mainstreamed evaluation in business, education, government, and nonprofit organizations.* That way, we can point to organizations that are successful *because of* their evaluation practices, as well as learn from their mistakes.
- *Develop a program of support for universities, associations, and organizations that are trying to move evaluation into the mainstream.* This program should include publications and qualified consultants who are experienced with mainstreaming evaluation in different kinds of organizations. Support could come from a nonprofit organization, a foundation, a university, or an association. It can and should be done.

References

Joint Committee on Standards for Educational Evaluation. *The Program Evaluation Standards.* Thousand Oaks, Calif.: Sage, 1994.

Sanders, J. R. "Presidential Address: On Mainstreaming Evaluation." *American Journal of Evaluation,* 2002, 23(3), 253–259.

Scriven, M. *Evaluation Thesaurus.* (4th ed.) Thousand Oaks, Calif.: Sage, 1991.

JAMES R. SANDERS is professor emeritus of educational studies at Western Michigan University. He served as associate director of the Evaluation Center at WMU from 1975 until his retirement in 2001, chaired the Joint Committee on Standards for Educational Evaluation from 1988 until 1998, and was president of the AEA in 2001.

2

Approaches to mainstreaming evaluation that appear to be successful in New Zealand, particularly in human services programs that serve both European and Maori populations, are presented. Three key elements are (1) to use an appropriate evaluation model, (2) to develop evaluation skills appropriate for each level of an organization, and (3) to use organization- or sector-level strategizing to identify priority evaluation questions.

Mainstreaming Evaluation or Building Evaluation Capability? Three Key Elements

Paul Duignan

One thing about being an evaluator working in New Zealand is that even if you follow the literature you get a sense of isolation from the debates happening within the evaluation discipline in the United States. At the same time, somewhat paradoxically, you draw extensively on much of that literature in order to inform your methodologies and approaches.

The author acknowledges Sally Casswell and the staff of the Alcohol and Public Health Research Unit (APHRU), University of Auckland, who are now working at the Centre for Social and Health Outcomes Research and Evaluation (SHORE), Massey University; Maori Kaumatua (Elder) Nau Epiha; Helen Moewaka Barnes and the staff of Whariki, its partner Maori research group; the organizational development company Navigate; John F. Smith and David Thomas, University of Waikato doctorate supervisors for part of this work, and Nan Wehipeihana, Maori evaluation colleague. Thanks as well to the hundreds of public health and community organization workers who have been involved in evaluation workshops and the New Zealand government funders of parts of this work: the New Zealand Health Research Council, Alcohol Advisory Council, Health Funding Authority, Ministry of Health, Ministry of Transport, and Ministry of Education.

Colleagues from the APHRU, SHORE, and Whariki involved in this evaluation work have also included Helen Moewaka Barnes (director, Whariki), Megan Tunks, Gayl Humphrey, Kim Conway, Belinda Borell, Bridgette Masters, Wendy Henwood, Alison Greenaway, Carla Spinola, Julie Macdonald, Wendy Epiha, Paul Stanley, Karen Witten, Lisa Morice, Jeff Adams, Tim McCreanor, Liz Stewart, Anaru Waa, Brendan Dacey, Allan Wyllie, Andy Thompson, John Benseman, Anton Turner, Francesca Holibar, Mary Anne Dehar, Maggie Jakob-Hoff, Naina Watene-Haydon, Jan Sheeran, Rachael Lane, Heather Seal, and Lisa Morice.

Evaluation as a discipline here is relatively tiny and has been shaped by both the size of the country (4 million, about the size of a number of cities in the United States) and the particular demands of our system of government administration. Our size creates various constraints on our work as evaluators; one is that our evaluation budgets are generally small by U.S. standards. Often programs and policies are introduced nationally, so there is no sense in which comparison communities (as in different states) can be used to evaluate outcomes. Even where programs are introduced locally and evaluation designs are set up, the programs often attract publicity (word-of-mouth networking), which can contaminate comparison groups.

On the positive side, evaluators, along with everyone else in a small country, are forced to be multiskilled generalists; we have to work closely with other professionals. It is relatively easy to network with a large proportion of the stakeholders from any sector one is working in, and access to senior policymakers is not particularly difficult, compared with larger countries. In addition, New Zealand has a working (there is a variety of opinion on how well it is working) treaty between the European population and the indigenous Maori—the Treaty of Waitangi. This relationship has forced us to start to come to terms with the power dynamic in evaluation and to try to develop appropriate ways of evaluating Maori programs. Although there are still many politics and practicalities to sort out on this issue, there have been some positive developments. In particular, the recognition that there needs to be more real autonomy for Maori to evaluate programs in ways that are appropriate for them. In addition, many lessons have been learned about evaluating community-based programs in the process. This chapter does not attempt to summarize all the extensive work that has been done by Maori in undertaking evaluations of programs for Maori in New Zealand and developing methodologies that work well with such programs. However, one example is given: the work undertaken by the Maori research group, Whariki, which works in partnership with my own research unit (Moewaka Barnes, 2000a, 2000b).

All this leaves some uncertainty as to what may or may not be relevant for North American evaluators from our unique perspective in New Zealand. I have been working in evaluation with Sally Casswell and other colleagues for the last fifteen years. These researchers were previously at the Alcohol and Public Health Research Unit (APHRU) at the University of Auckland and are now working at the Centre for Social and Health Outcomes Research and Evaluation (SHORE) at Massey University. During this time, we have had the luxury of working with one sector—those undertaking health promotion, public, and community health—to build evaluation capacity and capability in the sector as a whole. We have done this through developing appropriate models for evaluation, producing resources, running training programs at a range of different levels, and engaging with policymakers in discussions about approaches to evaluation. I was involved in much of the early work in this area and continue to have ongoing involvement. In addition, much of the teaching, research, and innovative work has been undertaken by the colleagues acknowledged elsewhere.

I was therefore interested to see that the Presidential Strand of the AEA's 2001 conference was on mainstreaming evaluation. In a sense, this is exactly what we have been trying to do for the public and community health sector over the decade and a half we have been working with it. On occasion, I have looked at the small size of the evaluation profession in New Zealand as a disadvantage to promoting evaluation in New Zealand. However, reflecting on the Presidential Strand theme, perhaps this has forced us to attempt to mainstream evaluation all along. We had no other strategy if we were to get any significant evaluation done in New Zealand. While, as specialist evaluators, we worked on a significant number of projects ourselves (and there were other evaluators working in the field), the bulk of evaluation needed to be done by those working in the sector itself if it was to be done at all.

A Perspective from Afar

The background paper for the Presidential Strand notes that the role of evaluation in organizations, including community agencies, government agencies, schools, and businesses has been marginalized in most cases (Sanders, 2002). It is always interesting to look back on the roots of a phenomenon. We might wonder, for example, how we have come to the point that evaluation is seen as being marginalized, at least in the United States. What has the situation looked like from a distance? Going back to the mid-1970s, when I was just starting to study evaluation and the evaluation heroes of the 1960s and 1970s were in vogue, it all seemed so straightforward. In those halcyon days, evaluation knew where it was going. We were building the "experimental society" of Donald Campbell (Campbell, 1975). Valiantly, we were applying what had been learned in the other sciences to large-scale evaluations of social programs. We just had to get the evaluations done and feed them through the appropriate political and policy channels so that the results could be implemented. We were well on the way to moving toward a modernist utopia—a place where increasingly rational, empirically based policymaking meant we had maximized our chances of achieving social policy goals.

Then along came Carol Weiss (1977), who pointed out that policymakers are driven by many different pressures in addition to our hard-won empirical evaluation results. She scaled our expectations back to the concept of enlightenment—the gradual process of results seeping through into decision making through various channels. But let's face it: enlightenment was a definite second best when we thought we were going to get direct traction on decision making through delivering policymakers "the facts." So evaluation got its first lesson in marginalization: we were only one voice among many in the decision-making process. Our initial expectation that we would take center stage in the decision-making process (be mainstreamed, as it were) was not met, and we had to develop a more sophisticated view of how we, as evaluators, could influence policymaking.

In any event, we still had our empirical methods; we could continue with collecting objective data, and in time it might ultimately flow through to policymakers and influence their decisions. Then we got hit by postmodernism, as it started to systematically deconstruct traditional quantitative objective social science and, by implication, evaluation. Philosophy of science issues have always loomed large in evaluation, as many of us had staked our reputations on our knowledge claims being somehow objective—or at least more objective than the multitude of subjective stakeholder claims being made for and against programs and policies. Guba and Lincoln (1989) led the charge with their view that knowledge was socially constructed, in contrast to the view that objective truth could be discovered. This was a problem, in that many of us had seen evaluators' unique professional mission as getting the facts to managers and policymakers. Here we had evaluators questioning whether we were ever going to be able to get objective hard data that were valid, reliable, and generalizable, and, most important, uncontestable.

In addition, indigenous people the world over—African Americans in the United States and other groups who have been truly marginalized to the fringes of economic, social, and political life—started to emerge from having been silenced by the previous centuries of colonialism and exploitation in its various guises. They highlighted the monocultural origins of the methods, concepts, and approaches being used in research and evaluation and pointed to the role of evaluation and research in the politics of oppression (Smith, 2000). In addition to this being a general challenge to evaluation, it was particularly telling in that many of the participants in the social programs that evaluators were working on were indigenous people or members of other marginalized groups.

The idea of seeing evaluation as an objective fact-finding exercise in the Western scientific tradition was accompanied by the realization that there were multiple stakeholders involved in any evaluation. In addition, a value judgment was required in order to determine which stakeholders' worldviews should be reflected in any evaluation. Some pushed this perspective right through to the point of arguing that evaluation should be all about value judgments in favor of particular stakeholders and opting for a process of empowerment for those involved in programs (Fetterman, Kaftarian, and Wandersman, 1996). Indigenous people, as the central stakeholders for many social programs, started to develop methods for undertaking evaluations that were consistent with their cultural traditions (Moewaka Barnes, 2000a, 2000b). All of this turmoil and debate resulted in a massive increase in the number of potential approaches and techniques available to evaluators. All of the qualitative and interpretative techniques from social science became available as legitimate evaluation methods standing alongside the quantitative techniques that had been honed by evaluation in the 1960s and 1970s.

While the repertoire of techniques expanded, the debate about approaches continued. Some valiantly maintained that there was the possibility of a workable objectivity in evaluations (Scriven, 1997). Others adopted the middle ground, arguing in a pragmatic fashion for "utilization focused" evaluation, which took as its starting point the various audiences for evaluation and had the evaluator simply work out which audiences they were working for and then design their evaluations to meet their needs (Patton, 1986). With this emphasis on meeting the needs of diverse stakeholder audiences, formative evaluation (improving program implementation) and process evaluation (describing program processes) took their place alongside outcome evaluation in the evaluator's repertoire. By the end of the last century, evaluation had a range of sophisticated quantitative and qualitative tools for evaluating programs that recognized the complexity of social programs, the epistemological and design issues that needed to be faced, and the diversity of stakeholders involved. In addition, in at least some contexts, evaluation had started to address the complex issue of evaluation approaches appropriate for indigenous peoples and other cultural groups. Evaluators were ready to take on the world; the world should have been calling out for evaluation to be mainstreamed.

Then what happened in the 1990s? Particularly in the United States, from my reading of the literature, large sections of the policy community completely ignored the sophistication of our profession and headed off independently into the performance management movement (Blalock, 1999). This is the often naïve attempt to measure a range of indicators and use them (with little regard to attributing causality) for holding social programs to account—a sort of ersatz outcomes evaluation with none of the sophistication we had spent decades of hard work developing. To some extent, evaluators were left in the role of sideline critics, complaining that the efforts being undertaken in performance management were too simplistic (Greene, 1999)—this while the policymakers and performance measurement people got on with the party, usually in blissful ignorance of the difficulty of what they were claiming they were going to be able to achieve. Marginalization for evaluation appeared again, ironically, this time not through having a too simplistic view of the world but through having a too sophisticated view of what could and could not be achieved in measuring programs and policies. So, given this history, what should evaluation as a discipline now do in the face of marginalization this time around? The obvious answer, given by the AEA 2001 Presidential Strand theme, is to try once again to mainstream evaluation.

What Mainstreaming Means

In looking at what is meant by mainstreaming evaluation, it is important to start by thinking about what we are trying to achieve by mainstreaming. We can start thinking about this by using the traditional formative evaluator's trick of "looking behind" the strategy we are proposing—mainstreaming evaluation, in this case. What is the goal that such mainstreaming is attempting to achieve? Presumably, the purpose of mainstreaming evaluation is to get our organizations, policies, and programs to be more effective and efficient. We can work back from our goal using a program logic approach and ask, What is needed to achieve this goal? Presumably, what's needed is that people at all levels throughout our organizations and policymaking processes are being more evaluative about what they do. Note that this does not mean they all need to be calling what they do *evaluation*. They simply need to ensure that people become more *evaluative*. They must have appropriate evaluation skills, systems, structures, and resources to support them in taking a more evaluative approach to their work.

Looked at this way, the task of mainstreaming evaluation may be better put as one of *building evaluative capability, building evaluation capacity*, or even *building an evaluation culture* throughout our programs, organizations, and policy development. Such evaluative activity may not necessarily be labeled evaluation but it should contribute to the goal of being more evaluative and making organizations, policies, and programs more effective and efficient.

At first sight, this idea of building evaluation capability appears to be synonymous with mainstreaming evaluation. Whether or not it is, however, depends on exactly what evaluators mean when they use the term *mainstreaming evaluation*. In my view, the term implies that we are trying once again to put evaluation at center stage. As evaluators, we need to think through the extent to which our desire to mainstream evaluation is an attempt to grow the profession, in contrast to simply getting people to be more evaluative. Looking at it as the attempt to get people to be more evaluative, we may need to be prepared to give evaluation away in order to build evaluation capability. *Giving evaluation away* means sharing skills and approaches without these necessarily being labeled as evaluation by those who use them. This is in contrast to looking for opportunities for growing the size and power of the evaluation profession.

In a sense, the growth of evaluation as a profession may be part of the cause for its marginalization. Professionalization of evaluation can reify evaluation and make it a separate activity that may or may not be "done" to programs. People ask, Are we going to do an evaluation of this program? This question implies that they need to decide whether or not they will call evaluators in to do a separate piece of work. Ideally, people should see evaluation as a central task they own themselves, and they may or may not have to involve outside evaluators in various aspects of what should be seen as a core task for the business as a whole.

All of this is not to imply that the evaluation profession should not continue and, in fact, thrive. There are enormous technical challenges in designing some types of evaluation, and specialist evaluators will always have to be involved in these. All that is being argued here is that the most useful strategy in attempting to mainstream evaluation is probably to try and give it way rather than expect that evaluation, as an entity, can be mainstreamed.

So how can we go about giving evaluation away or building evaluation capacity in our organizations? I have been working on this question over the last decade and a half in New Zealand. In the 1980s, working with Sally Casswell and colleagues at the University of Auckland in the health promotion, public, and community health field, we became interested in the best way to build evaluation capability for the sector as a whole. We ran a large number of training workshops for people from various parts of the sector and undertook and consulted on the methodology for many evaluations. The author was involved in a number of these, and many others were undertaken by colleagues at the APHRU, who now work at SHORE, and by Whariki, the Maori research unit working in partnership with the APHRU (now SHORE). From my experience working with these university colleagues and from working as a consultant evaluator in a number of other sectors outside health, I believe that three key elements are required to build evaluation capability. Each of these is discussed next.

Elements of Building Evaluation Capability

The three key elements of building evaluation capacity are as follows:

1. Using an appropriate evaluation model
2. Developing evaluation skills appropriate for each level of an organization or sector through a range of training opportunities
3. Organization- or sector-level strategizing to identify priority evaluation questions rather than rely on evaluation planning at the individual program level

Using an Appropriate Evaluation Model. The first element in building evaluation capacity is using an appropriate evaluation model. Although this may seem a slightly obscure and theoretical place to start thinking about building evaluation capability, it is important to think about the most useful way of describing evaluation for the purpose of building evaluation capability. There are a number of different ways in which evaluation can be described and a number of different typologies that are used (Rossi and Freeman, 1989; Chelimsky and Shadish, 1997). Terms used for types of evaluation include *quasi-experimental design* (Cook and Campbell, 1979), *formative* (McClintock, 1986), *developmental, implementation, process, impact, outcome, summative, stakeholder, empowerment* (Fetterman, Kaftarian, and Wandersman, 1996), *goal-free* (Scriven, 1991), *utilization-focused* (Patton, 1986), *fourth generation* (Guba and Lincoln, 1989), and *naturalistic* (Guba, 1978; Guba and Lincoln, 1981). As in any discipline, these terms describe various conceptual levels and are used in various ways by various evaluators for various purposes. So what type of evaluation model or typology is the most appropriate for building evaluation capability?

It is useful to identify a set of criteria to determine which models are the most appropriate for building evaluation capacity. I have developed a provisional list of criteria, which are set out in Table 2.1. For each of the criteria, I have briefly described how I think the model used in our capacity-building work meets the criteria. More detailed discussion of these points can be found in Duignan (2002).

Developing Skills. The second step in building evaluation capacity is to develop skills, systems, and structures for evaluation activity at all levels within organizations and within a sector. From my experience in the New Zealand context (and this may well apply in the United States and other countries), there is a lack of both an adequate conceptualization of and skills in evaluation across all organizational levels. Policymakers, funders, service provider management, staff, and program participants tend to have a relatively limited understanding of evaluation. If they have more than this, it has often been based, at least until recently, on the erroneous view that evaluation is limited to outcome evaluation.

The objective of skills development in evaluation for an organization or sector is to further sophistication about evaluation and to teach appropriate evaluation skills to those who can use them in their day-to-day work. This can be done by developing manuals and training resources and by running training workshops.

My colleagues and I developed a series of manuals over a decade that reflect this model and have been widely distributed throughout the public and community health sector in New Zealand (Casswell and Duignan, 1989; Duignan, Dehar, and Casswell, 1992; Turner and others, 1992; Waa, Holibar, and Spinola, 1998). These manuals deliberately copied the visual style of an early key sector document on health promotion (New Zealand Board of Health Committee on Health Promotion, 1988), so they would be seen as having continuity with sector documents rather than being "evaluation" documents external to the sector. As time has gone on, the response to these manuals has been evaluated and subsequent versions have been amended on the basis of this feedback. Currently, the Maori research group Whariki is developing one of these manuals specifically for evaluating programs for Maori.

During the period of time that the resources have been available, the APHRU (now SHORE) and Whariki have carried out a series of training workshops for different audiences within the sector. The different types of training are

- *Brief presentations on evaluation at a range of sector workshops on other issues.* Typically, these last for one to two hours and cover the general evaluation model and principles, as well as raise awareness of evaluation within the sector.

Table 2.1. Criteria to Determine Which Evaluation Models Are the Most Appropriate

Criteria for an Evaluation Model Suitable for Capacity Building	*Features of the Evaluation Model Used in This Case*
Demystifies evaluation	Evaluation was conceptualized and taught as fundamentally asking a simple question: Is this [organizational activity, policy, program] being done in the best possible way? The question can then be broken down into three subsidiary areas: (1) How can we improve it? (2) How can we describe the course and context of it? and (3) What have been the positive and negative, intended and unintended, outcomes from it? Feedback from training based on this model was that using it had significantly demystified evaluation for the participants.
Uses a set of evaluation terms that emphasize that evaluation can take place right across a program's lifecycle and is not limited to outcome evaluation.	The evaluation model used the terms formative, process, and outcome evaluation, which correspond to the three subsidiary questions. This was in contrast to models that distinguish just two terms (for example, formative versus summative or process versus outcome). This model allows project staff and management to see a role for themselves in doing evaluation and, equally important, allows evaluation resources to be used at all points of the program lifecycle. Further discussion of the advantages of this typology can be found in Duignan (2003).
Allows a role for both internal and external evaluators	The model allowed for both internal and external evaluators and provided many examples of simple evaluation techniques that could be used by program staff and management.
Has methods for hard-to-evaluate, real-world programs, not just for ideal, large-scale, expensive, external evaluation designs	The model included techniques for evaluating real-world multistrategy community programs with wide-ranging outcomes (Duignan and Casswell, 1992; Duignan, 1997; Duignan and others, 2002).
Does not privilege any one meta-approach to evaluation (for example, goal-free, empowerment)	Evaluation meta-approaches are high-level philosophies and guiding principles for the way evaluations should be conducted (for example, goal-free, empowerment evaluation). These can be distinguished conceptually from evaluation purposes, methods, and designs (Duignan, 2003). The evaluation model used in this capacity building accepted a range of possible evaluation approaches and did not endorse one to the exclusion of others.

- *Two-day Level I courses for service provider, lower-level managers and staff.* Participants can discuss the overall evaluation model and learn specific evaluation skills that they can use in their day-to-day work. Considerable time is spent demystifying evaluation and describing simple formative and process evaluation methods that can be used by service provider staff. Outcome evaluation methods are discussed, including how to recognize when outside evaluation expertise is needed.
- *More advanced, Level II two-day courses for service provider managers and staff wanting to further develop their skills.* These courses provide more in-depth training in evaluation.
- *One-week workshops for policymakers, funders, larger provider specialists, and researchers to develop and practice appropriate evaluation skills.* These workshops cover the evaluation model and the skills and techniques discussed in the Level I and II workshops in more depth, with further discussion of outcome evaluation issues.
- *Workshops specifically run by Maori evaluators for Maori program management and staff.* These workshops look at evaluation concepts and methods from a Maori perspective.
- *One-day overview workshops to discuss evaluation concepts and approaches for service provider management.* These workshops discuss the concepts from the evaluation model and how these relate to organizational policies and practices. Examples: distinguishing between performance management and evaluation, discovering what is and is not realistic to expect in terms of outcome evaluation, and setting organizational priorities for evaluation.
- *One-day workshops for staff and management within an organization.* This is an opportunity to discuss the model, concepts in evaluation, and the idea of prioritizing evaluation questions across the organization as a whole.
- *Postgraduate university master's papers.* Papers may be written by researchers and practitioners interested in further developing their understanding of evaluation and their ability to undertake evaluations.

All of these courses, apart from the managers' courses, involve discussion of evaluation models, combined with hands-on work with evaluation projects brought to the workshops by participants. This action-learning approach ensures that participants go away with a feeling of mastery in at least some evaluation techniques, which further assists in promoting the idea that some aspects of evaluation can be done by people at all levels within a program, organization, or sector.

The idea is that the end result of this ongoing activity will be a sector that (1) has a much more sophisticated model of evaluation, (2) is in a position to talk sensibly about evaluation questions within the sector, and (3) all levels within the sector know how to undertake some evaluation tasks appropriate to their work situation.

Strategizing About How to Prioritize Evaluation Questions. The third and final element in building evaluation capacity is to encourage organizational or sector strategizing about what are priority evaluation questions. The current problem is not that too little evaluation is being done in a sector. Funders may be routinely demanding evaluation, and service providers may be having evaluations done. The problem is whether evaluation resources are being used in the most efficient way possible. Current practice in New Zealand, which may well be the case in the United States, is that the steps that are described next happen.

An evaluator gets called in to advise on evaluation methodology for a program. Often there are enough resources to "do an evaluation." The problem is that little thought or guidance is offered by funders or others in the organization or sector as to what the evaluation questions should be or how they might be prioritized.

In theory, of course, the evaluator can use one of the stakeholder evaluations or related approaches and consult with the various stakeholders about what they see as the priority questions for evaluating the program. All evaluators do this to some extent. The problem is that it does not really make sense to do this repeatedly on a program-by-program basis, particularly when such programs are relatively small. The program in question may or may not be a priority for evaluation. The evaluation resources may be better spent elsewhere, and perhaps only a small-scale evaluation should be undertaken for the program in question. For instance, it may be a well-established program for which (contrary to many instances) good formative evaluation has already been carried out and previous work on a similar program has shown positive outcomes. It may be better to spend the evaluation resources that are available on an entirely different initiative that explores new ways of dealing with the social issue the original program is attempting to address.

The key point is that there should be no assumption that any particular type or scale of evaluation is suitable for all programs. Unfortunately, this assumption often underlies the notion that a program "needs an evaluation." The assumption, for funders at least, is usually that this will consist of an outcome evaluation that will accurately determine whether the program has met its objectives or not. In my experience, funders usually give little thought to how feasible or expensive an outcome evaluation may be; they just pass the problem on to the service provider management, staff, and any evaluation specialists they employ.

Of course, in addition to evaluation in the sense being used here, all programs need basic monitoring as to whether they are on track using cheap, routinely measured performance indicators. This is usually best dealt with as a separate process that can be linked to more complex evaluations when these are undertaken. The essential distinction is that *monitoring* should be undertaken on a routine basis for accountability, and *evaluation,* because of its higher cost, should be used on a more selective, strategic basis.

In contrast to the current, program-focused approach to evaluation planning, there should be an organization- or sector-based approach to evaluation question prioritization. Rather than simply saying that every program needs an evaluation, it would be more fruitful to ask, How can we best spend our evaluation resources to answer priority evaluation questions for this organization or this sector? This second question is particularly useful if it is put in terms of strategic planning for the future rather than as a futile attempt to use evaluation as a routine method for measuring accountability—something I suspect at least part of the performance management movement has yet to discover.

I have been working with the approach advocated here in the context of organization-level policy-setting exercises, which occur when an organization develops an explicit evaluation policy as a preliminary step to introducing a more strategic approach to the program-based evaluation work already being undertaken. Typically, these policies contain elements such as these:

- The evaluation models that will be used in the organization
- Policies regarding and opportunities for staff training in evaluation
- Sources of and procedures for obtaining technical evaluation assistance
- Procedures and stakeholder consultation standards for evaluation planning and sign-off
- Procedures and consultation processes regarding cultural issues
- Guidelines on the typical scope and type of evaluation for different sizes and types of programs
- Guidelines on the use of internal and external evaluators
- Ethical and other, related considerations
- Policies about disclosure of evaluation information

In addition, some progress has been made in helping organizations to prioritize the evaluation questions they are asking of the programs they are running. When I have been involved in such instances, the process has been fairly tentative.

Of course, in most instances one organization's programs are just part of the overall activity in a sector. It is even more useful then for prioritization of evaluation to take place at the sector rather than at the organization level. In an ideal world, sectors would have systems that give them the opportunity to reflect on the priority evaluation questions. They would then get an indication of the cost of answering these questions and move to make strategic decisions about which type of evaluations for which programs should and should not take place. This views the evaluation costs for a whole sector as one large research and development fund that needs to be spent wisely, rather than make evaluation decisions on a program-by-program basis. This is not to say that people from the program level should have no input into the development of the evaluation questions; it's just that input should not all be left to that level.

Of course, it can be argued that already a lot of organizational and sector strategic considerations are factored into the evaluation requirements for an individual program. Funders will indicate which programs they want to have evaluated and what the level of resources is; they may indicate which evaluation questions they want answered. In addition, in reviews of the academic literature and in priority-setting processes within research funding bodies, prioritization does occur. In sectors where there are ongoing research groups involved in teaching, advising, and undertaking a large number of evaluations, those groups play a role through having a strategic view of a sector and determining which evaluation questions are the next priority. My research colleagues and I have played this role to some extent in our sector. However, I would argue that this process is still too ad hoc and that there is often a disjunction between priority setting (when it is taking place) and what actually happens on the ground in regard to the evaluation of the many programs that are subject to evaluation. Facilitating such prioritization work could be a major contribution of evaluators to building evaluation capability.

Exactly how to facilitate this cross-organizational or sector prioritization is a difficult question. Sectors dealing with social issues tend to be made up of a diverse range of public and private groups funding a diverse range of programs. Some innovative priority-setting exercises are going on in New Zealand at the moment in the labor and employment program area (K. McKegg, personal communication, 2000). In addition, I am working with other sectors in an attempt to get this sort of prioritization process to occur. It would be interesting to look at models that have been developed to facilitate such priority setting in other areas. More detailed information on the issue of being strategic about evaluation can be found at www.strategicevaluation.info.

Conclusion

In this chapter, I have examined the concept of mainstreaming evaluation. I have drawn on my experiences largely within the health promotion, public, and community health and related social sectors in New Zealand. In the New Zealand public and community health sector, we have made more progress on the first two (models and training rather than sector prioritizing) of the three key elements for building evaluation capability described here.

My intention has been to generate some points for discussion around the issue of mainstreaming evaluation. The questions, among others, that I suggest include the following:

In mainstreaming, is there a difference between building the evaluation profession and giving evaluation way?

Are the models of evaluation used in mainstreaming important? If so, are the criteria suggested in this chapter the right ones? What models are likely to be best for discussing evaluation with nonevaluation audiences?

Can we further develop evaluation approaches that can deal with the realities of on-the-ground programs and community-based programs rather than just use textbook evaluation designs for "ideal" programs?

How can evaluators support the development of indigenous peoples' and other groups' evaluation models and approaches?

What are innovative methods of training for mainstreaming evaluation?

How can organization- and sector-level prioritization exercises for evaluation questions be encouraged? Is there a particular role for evaluators in facilitating these processes?

References

Blalock, A. "Evaluation Research and the Performance Management Movement." *Evaluation,* 1999, *5*(2), 117–149.

Campbell, D. T. "Reforms as Experiments." In E. L. Struening and M. Guttentag (eds.), *Handbook of Evaluation Research.* Thousand Oaks, Calif.: Sage, 1975.

Casswell, S., and Duignan, P. *Evaluating Health Promotion: A Guide for Health Promoters and Health Managers.* Auckland, New Zealand: Department of Community Health, School of Medicine, University of Auckland, 1989.

Chelimsky, E., and Shadish, W. R. (eds.). *Evaluation for the Twenty-First Century: A Handbook.* Thousand Oaks, Calif.: Sage, 1997.

Cook, T., and Campbell, D. T. *Quasi-Experimentation: Design and Analysis Issues for Field Settings.* Boston: Houghton Mifflin, 1979.

Duignan, P. "Evaluating Health Promotion: The Strategic Evaluation Framework." Unpublished doctoral dissertation, University of Waikato, Hamilton, New Zealand, 1997.

Duignan, P. "Building Social Policy Evaluation Capacity." *Social Policy Journal of New Zealand,* 2002, *19,* 197–198.

Duignan, P. "Approaches and Terminology in Programme and Policy Evaluation." In N. Lunt, C. Davidson, and K. McKegg (eds.), *Evaluating Policy and Practice: A New Zealand Reader.* Auckland: Pearson Education, 2003.

Duignan, P., and Casswell, S. "Community Alcohol Action Programmes Evaluation in New Zealand." *Journal of Drug Issues,* 1992, 22, 757–771.

Duignan, P. S., and others. *Community Project Indicators Framework (CPIF) Working Draft.* Wellington, New Zealand: New Zealand Ministry of Health, 2002. [http://www.moh.govt.nz/moh.nsf/49ba80c00757b8804c256673001d47d0/48f14012c1e6f9facc256ccd00083dd8/$FILE/CPIF0203.pdf].

Duignan, P., Dehar, M., and Casswell, S. *Planning Evaluation of Health Promotion Programmes: A Framework for Decision Making.* Auckland: Alcohol and Public Health Research Unit, School of Medicine, University of Auckland, 1992.

Fetterman, D., Kaftarian, S., and Wandersman, A. *Empowerment Evaluation: Knowledge and Tools for Self-Assessment and Accountability.* Thousand Oaks, Calif.: Sage, 1996.

Greene, J. "The Inequality of Performance Measurements." *Evaluation,* 1999, *5*(2), 160–172.

Guba, E. G. *Toward a Methodology of Naturalistic Inquiry in Educational Evaluation.* Los Angeles: Center for the Study of Evaluation, University of California, Los Angeles, 1978.

Guba, E. G., and Lincoln, Y. S. *Effective Evaluation: Improving the Usefulness of Evaluation Results Through Responsive and Naturalistic Approaches.* San Francisco: Jossey-Bass, 1981.

Guba, E. G., and Lincoln, Y. S. *Fourth Generation Evaluation.* Thousand Oaks, Calif.: Sage, 1989.

McClintock, C. "Towards a Theory of Formative Program Evaluation." *Evaluation Studies Review Annual,* 1986, *11,* 205–223.

Moewaka Barnes, H. "Collaboration in Community Action, a Successful Partnership Between Indigenous Communities and Researchers." *Health Promotion International,* 2000a, *15,* 17–25.

Moewaka Barnes, H. "Kaupapa Maori: Explaining the Ordinary." *Pacific Health Dialog,* 2000b, *7*(1), 13–16.

New Zealand Board of Health Committee on Health Promotion. *Promoting Health in New Zealand.* Wellington: New Zealand Board of Health, 1988.

Patton, M. Q. *Utilization Focused Evaluation.* Thousand Oaks, Calif.: Sage, 1986.

Rossi, P. H., and Freeman, H. E. *Evaluation: A Systematic Approach.* Thousand Oaks, Calif.: Sage, 1989.

Sanders, J. R. "Presidential Address: On Mainstreaming Evaluation." *American Journal of Evaluation,* 2002, *23*(3), 253–259.

Scriven, M. *Evaluation Thesaurus.* Thousand Oaks, Calif.: Sage, 1991.

Scriven, M. "Truth and Objectivity in Evaluation." In E. Chelimsky and W. R. Shadish (eds.), *Evaluation for the Twenty-First Century: A Handbook.* Thousand Oaks, Calif.: Sage, 1997.

Smith, L. T. *Decolonising Methodology: Research and Indigenous Peoples.* London: Zed Books, 2000.

Turner, A., Dehar, M., Casswell, S., and MacDonald, J. *Doing Evaluation: A Manual for Health Promotion Workers.* Auckland: Alcohol and Public Health Research Unit, University of Auckland, 1992.

Waa, A., Holibar, F., and Spinola, C. *Programme Evaluation: An Introductory Guide for Health Promotion.* Auckland: Alcohol and Public Health Research Unit/Whariki, University of Auckland, 1998.

Weiss, C. "Research for Policy's Sake: The Enlightenment Function of Social Research." *Policy Analysis,* 1977, *3,* 531–545.

PAUL DUIGNAN is a senior research fellow at the Centre for Social and Health Outcomes Research and Evaluation, Massey University, Auckland, New Zealand, and works for Parker Duignan Ltd. as an evaluation methodologist and strategic planner.

3

Mainstreaming evaluation requires establishing aesthetic and ethical frameworks, as well as developing knowledge and skills that make "doing evaluation" seem like the right thing. Mainstreaming, however, can pose challenges to good evaluation practice; a view from cultural anthropology suggests that evaluation can have distinct meanings in different settings. Stories from program evaluation research in Indonesia illustrate the ways comforts and rigidities associated with mainstreamed evaluation processes may hinder high-quality evaluation.

The Rigidity and Comfort of Habits: A Cultural and Philosophical Analysis of the Ups and Downs of Mainstreaming Evaluation

Nancy Grudens-Schuck

The concept of mainstreaming presents a series of interesting dilemmas. I do not intend to use this space to strongly reject or endorse mainstreaming, either as a concept or as a phenomenon. Mainstreaming happens, it needs to happen, and that is a credit to dedicated and astute evaluators working in many fields. Instead, I offer the reader an opportunity to think philosophically and culturally about the phenomenon of mainstreaming.

I approach evaluation from the perspective of cultural anthropology, which means that I cannot avoid viewing evaluation as a cultural event. My remarks are very much an "anthropology of evaluation." I am also comfortable introducing my ideas through stories—something anthropologists like to do. This story centers around a trip to Indonesia in January 2000.

Indonesia, January 2000

I secured funds to travel to several islands in eastern Indonesia to witness a large-scale participatory evaluation of an exemplary conservation and development project (Fisher, Moeliono, and Wodicka, 1998). I intended to learn

I was encouraged by Robert Martin, Jack Barnette, and Susan Boser while developing the chapter, which is based on a presentation at the annual meeting of the AEA in 2001. Activities described in the article were funded by an Iowa State University (ISU) travel grant in 2000 and by the ISU agricultural experiment station and the State of Iowa.

how evaluation occurred in a large-scale project that had used participatory evaluation and action research throughout its development (Wodicka, 1999). My excitement was fueled by the idea of witnessing participatory evaluation in a cultural context that was strikingly different from that of my North American-based work. Participatory evaluation has many forms but, typically, features shared control of evaluation processes. Participatory evaluation also involves a wider range of stakeholders in collecting and assessing data than is usual in other approaches (Cousins and Whitmore, 1998).

I interviewed staff and researchers as we toured islands where villagers raised corn on rainforest hillsides, fished magnificent coral reefs, and complained about Komodo dragons eating their goats. Everywhere there was participation: participatory action research was taking place with villagers and government to address conflicts over forest boundaries; trainers and trainees were discussing participatory rural appraisal (Chambers, 1997), and social forestry projects were ongoing. I was privileged to meet participatory nongovernmental organization (NGO) facilitators and village leaders working to better the lives of people in a country that had seen many years of repression. As a self-professed participatory junkie, I was thrilled and wowed to make this trip.

The story takes a turn here. The turnabout surprised me—an example of my biases and assumptions tripping me up (again). My unsettling began as I asked about the project's participatory-evaluation-in-progress during personal interviews and continued through follow-up phone interviews six months later. It seems there were various complaints about the evaluation not being as participatory as people had hoped or as people were used to experiencing. An Indonesian national close to the project said, "I think that the evaluation of the consortium is not so participatory." A key staff person confirmed, "We just did an evaluation. We weren't the facilitators of it. We hired outside facilitators, but they were very open in terms of doing a participatory evaluation and really playing the role of facilitators rather than outside legal kind of evaluation and passing judgments." He later added, "The facilitators sometimes responded as evaluators and sometimes responded as facilitators. Sometimes they were really trying to influence the recommendations. They brought in their own biases, their own way of thinking about the network." The outsider process favored "recommendations rather than lessons learned." This produced difficult, "arduous discussions." Especially noteworthy was when evaluation facilitators asked for consensus on a key issue and received none, so they requested a vote. The vote was overturned the next day (after the facilitators had left). This story in particular portrayed an evaluation process that was less participatory than much of the consortium's ongoing evaluative work. The results were considered less beneficial and the process less than ideal.

This story is not remarkable in the disarray it reveals or even for its flip-flop processes. Moreover, the story is not unique in showing that evaluation is impure, complex, and socially constructed—features understood in the evaluation field (Patton, 1997). At first, I presumed that the failure to employ participatory processes had something to do with the participatory methods themselves. Perhaps participation was feared as dangerously political, too revealing. This enormous archipelago, as we are perhaps more aware than in years past, is the largest Muslim country in the world and continues to experience ethnic and religious conflict (Chambers, 1997; Mayer, 1996). Risks associated with methods of inquiry certainly occur in the real world. We ignore these risks at our own peril—more so the peril of our clients—for evaluations conducted in politically unstable areas of the world. I admit, however, that this preliminary, and perhaps romantic, analysis was colored by the we-would-be-martyrs syndrome that I sometimes exude when I witness the lukewarm reception of participatory techniques. But I do not think this was the right analysis. I think a better analysis has more to do with the effect of mainstreaming in evaluation and the way mainstreaming is another way to say "enculturated."

Culture and Evaluation

When something is enculturated, the event or behavior has meaning that is intimately connected to tacit webs of understanding, to paraphrase cultural anthropologist Clifford Geertz (1973). It is important that we consider that evaluation, like other events and behaviors, is part of culture and has been developed to have meanings particular to time and place. Such meanings include yet are beyond how evaluation professionals—cultural creatures themselves—define themselves and their activities. We may realize that clients, funders, and organizations are under the spell of conventions, histories, and traditions. It is frequently clear to us that others have cultures. I submit that we evaluators avoid, however, whole-hog analysis of ourselves and our activities as culture-bound. We admit *biases*, but these typically are portrayed as individual, as superficial, or as under our control. And so we are able to "bracket" them, as the jargon goes, and get on with the evaluation.

Ernie House and Ken Howe (1999) have pushed this line of thinking for us through their work on values in evaluation. They suggest that we consider two ways of managing key challenges in evaluation and that most employ reasoning that is information and lacking an explicit framework.

What is inside the black box of informal reasoning? I argue that culture is inside and is not just culture with a big "C." Commonly, one thinks about culture as long-standing historical and ethnic attributes like foods, mannerisms, and customs. Some in our community are also aware that honoring culture involves coming to terms with power (Guba and Lincoln, 1989; Rorty, 1982). In combination, these are important and essential dimensions of culture that press us unendingly. However, on an everyday basis, even when we believe we have figured out the big C stuff, there is always more culture knocking at the door. Notably, local *organizational cultures* occur in evaluation units as well as in client organizations. Such cultures are surprisingly common. It may be most practical to state that culture "writ large and small" must be considered when unpacking such terms as *informal reasoning*.

Eleanor Chelimsky and William Shadish (1997) acknowledge the force of culture, suggesting, "It is often uncomfortable to stir oneself from familiar cultural, topical, conceptual, and methodological niches." They end, "So we must face the discomfort of stirring ourselves if we are to avoid being left behind" (p. xiii). What is underdeveloped among us is the acknowledgment that we are *part* of culture; therefore, so is evaluation. We must not only avoid being left behind but must strive to avoid other unfortunate outcomes that result from ignoring *our* culture as well as *their* culture—outcomes such as gathering bad data, ignoring important stakeholders, and overestimating peoples' willingness to assist in evaluation. Such mistakes can contribute to an evaluation that violates professional standards (Joint Committee on Standards for Educational Evaluation, 1994).

Tacit Knowledge and Habits

This problem of not seeing culture may be inevitable. In anthropology, culture is talked about using an analogy based on fish and water. We say, "The fish is the last creature to see the water" to indicate the marvelous ability of people to fail to notice the rules that govern them (see also Bateson, 1980). In the professions, attending unconsciously to fundamentals is not all bad. Part of moving into a professional role is to learn to do the job so well that we do not have to think about it. Donald Schön (1983) enlightened us to the patterned ways in which informal and intuitive professional knowledge is both tacit and powerful. Personally, I like the feeling of moving seamlessly among tasks, zipping along, unencumbered by hesitation. The concept of *mainstreaming* can be viewed as a process that evaluators and organizations take for granted (Picciotto, 2002).

The Unconscious and the Unshakeable

Schön (1983) concluded that many of our professional ideas exist at an unconscious level. He also believed that many of the ideas held by professionals were nearly unshakable. Moreover, to the extent that evaluators are similar to other professionals, evaluators also possess ideas that are both unconscious and unshakeable. There is a downside to working from the heart or relying on one's gut instinct: when circumstances change, trouble begins. For example, when faced with *clear evidence* that their ideas weren't working, Schön and colleague Chris Argyris discovered that professionals typically dismiss the evidence (Argyris and Schön, 1996). Worse, the professionals who were able to accept the evidence failed to act differently, even when they pledged to do so. This may occur among evaluators as well.

Return to Evaluation in Indonesia

I return to the story of evaluation in Indonesia. The tip-off that evaluation was playing its cultural hand in the Indonesian setting was the lack of discussion about the pros and cons of participatory evaluation itself. For example, people did not talk about the risks of participatory evaluation, nor did people dwell on practical problems or benefits of participatory evaluation. Moreover, although situated in a nation very different from my own, neither outsiders nor insiders talked about the decision to use an outside evaluation process as "Indonesian" (a phrase that includes a multitude of cultures and languages) in any cultural sense.

Instead, people said they did not use participatory evaluation because it was the ten-year anniversary of the program. Apparently, for ten-year anniversary evaluations, a comprehensive, external evaluation felt right.

Now go figure. What would you do with this response?

Early on, I dismissed this "anniversary" explanation. It did not seem worth noticing. Why would a ten-year anniversary cause an organization with a remarkable history of participatory education and evaluation to opt for an outsider evaluation process heavy on recommendations? Nonetheless, continued discussions bore this out.

> Of course, "we were having had" ten years of this consortium. We were interested in knowing what kind of impact we have had so far. . . . we were interested in having a kind of independent team, people from the outside coming to the consortium and helping us identify what lessons we have learned from the work that we have been doing over the last ten years. . . . This was more or less like a ten year anniversary, where we wanted to set some time aside specifically for evaluation.

The notion of *anniversary* warrants unpacking. Anniversaries are complex and particular, but their cues are nearly always related to time, ritual, authority, and a reconstruction of "the story." This is not silly stuff. It is, in fact, culture. The prospect of ritual related to anniversaries is powerful, not just in Indonesia but in NGOs and in the workplace in the United States. After all, we would not have attended to the concept of mainstreaming as an AEA Presidential Strand event in 2001 if we were not at least partly susceptible to the impetus of celebration and ritual as conducted properly by President Sanders. Evaluation enacts culture at the same time that evaluation is an expression of culture.

Culture and Mainstreaming

The cultural view bears directly on the issue of mainstreaming. I can argue, for example, that evaluation of whatever stripe is mainstreamed when it becomes part of organizational culture. This is both good news and bad news. The good news is that once they are part of the culture, habits become regular. People enact cultures tacitly, naturally, intuitively. They do not have to think about it. Moreover, culture is durable, so once mainstreamed, evaluation sticks.

The bad news is that once mainstreamed, it is hard to change, even when change is warranted. For example, people's ideas about evaluation are often regrettable. Evaluation can be a way for a business to downsize. Evaluation can be used to unjustly remove particular people or programs. My students are appalled that many organizations distribute end-of-meeting forms with mechanical precision but mindless attention. Evaluation, in these cases, is perfunctory. Sometimes, one can scratch the surface of such an organization's lack of cooperation with evaluation protocols and discover that evaluation has been used to harass employees. Kalyani Rai (2001) learned that among her Asian immigrant clients, evaluation was equivalent to colonization. In such cases, resistance to evaluation makes more sense than cooperation.

When evaluators try to change these types of mainstreamed habits, one learns a lot about resistance and about power (Picciotto, 2002). Metaphors are avenues to understanding what evaluation means to different organizations, as noted in Patton's (2000) overview of the role of language in evaluation. He describes opening a meeting with new clients by eliciting their metaphors for evaluation. About eight years ago, I conducted an evaluation that clients repeatedly described as "ammunition" for their organization. More recently, a prospective client talked about evaluation as a "shield." Another described the role of evaluation as leading to a higher state of consciousness. Ammunition, shields, and enlightenment are distinct indeed. Such metaphors are crucial to understanding how clients see the role of the evaluator and are the key to understanding what evaluation already means in the setting.

A hallmark of habits is rigidity. Again, this is not so much judgment as it is a practical matter. It is an oxymoron to think of irregular habits or elusive habits. Habits are habits because they have integrity in their sameness, are well integrated with other parts of the culture, and resist change. Ideas about evaluation that are durable and deleterious to the progress of organizations, to public knowledge, and to accountability are regrettable. Rigidity can be problematic.

As we examine mainstreaming, we might benefit from consideration of the sister concepts of interruption and change. Under the right conditions, organizational habits can change. Understanding the process of change would help evaluators address several questions related to mainstreaming:

- How may evaluators successfully introduce new evaluation methods?
- What ideas about evaluation do clients hold tightly or lightly?
- How may evaluators help people unlearn outmoded habits related to evaluation?

- How will change affect people and ideas that are currently "in power"?
- How might evaluators help organizations institutionalize evaluation protocols in ways that prevent relapse, especially in the face of key staff or leadership turnover?
- What are the limits of training, for ourselves and others, with respect to habits of evaluation that are tacit and rigid?

Remember that the flip side of this issue acknowledges mainstreaming as potentially healthy. Mainstreamed habits reduce thinking. I am fine with that. However, as my colleague Lynn Jones tells his students, evaluators are charged with *causing thinking and learning* when they enter an evaluation context (personal communication, 2000). Evaluation is a social intervention (Guba and Lincoln, 1989). It is a way to assist people to interact or process in nontrivial ways (Bateson, 1980). Evaluation can be an opportunity to structure relationships differently so that the necessary conversations can occur and people can learn. We are change agents, provocateurs, animators when we do our jobs well.

Possibility for Change

I will not present a comprehensive framework for change of people and organizations; there are many good theories. I will simply touch on a few key concepts. First, educational psychology suggests that difference and disorientation are necessary for thinking "outside the box." The concept of unfreezing-freezing, developed by social psychologist Kurt Lewin (1948), is instructive here. Lewin studied how people might institute new practices in industry and in the home. Lewin knew that habits undermine change, even when change made sense or was expected to help, so he coined the terms *unfreezing-freezing* to suggest that new learning had to be preceded by a period of *un*learning. Adult educators continue to find these concepts useful. Adults who need to change usually know the technical aspects of change but don't know how to make it happen.

Lewin (1948) further discovered that learning and unlearning were not interchangeable; people do not substitute one concept for another. Rather, in the phase of unfreezing, concepts are loosened and muddled, hence the slushy metaphor. The contemporary term *constructivism* now enfolds such concepts (Guba and Lincoln, 1989). A constructivist framework assumes that people create new knowledge based on prior knowledge. Specific, even confrontational methods are required to get people to *unlearn what they already know* about evaluation, marriage, the Internet, Aunt Pearl, anthrax, Toronto, or anything else. Adult educator Jack Mezirow (1991) documented the essential role of a disorienting dilemma in catalyzing significant learning. The mistake is to pour new knowledge over old and expect long-lasting change.

Pragmatism, Habits, and Mainstreaming

John Dewey (1938) and modern neopragmatist philosophers like Richard Rorty (1982) present habits as steady yet tentative. There is always the possibility for change. Dewey's notion of "settled knowledge" advocates for a view of behavior and beliefs as susceptible to change, even when they seem "rock hard." For Dewey, there was no final knowledge, no pure essence of truth. These beliefs are what make him a pragmatist, not in the sense of being simplistic or superficial but as a cofounder of a philosophy that dismisses the search for perfect truth (Langsdorf and Smith, 1995).

The implications of pragmatist ideas for the concept of mainstreaming in evaluation are two-fold. On the one hand, evaluation can be tentative yet not seem that way because there is a great advantage to viewing settled knowledge (or conditions) as firm and actionable. Additionally, a pragmatist view would emphasize that mainstreamed evaluation practices are enmeshed in present time, situated in particular contexts. As contexts change and as beliefs become unsettled, what is currently mainstreamed may become habits that we later hope are unlearned. Of course, we live this tension in the AEA. Egon Guba and Yvonna Lincoln's *Fourth Generation Evaluation* (1989) made some in the evaluation community squirm and become disoriented. Perhaps Guba and Lincoln's strong claims accomplished Lewin's *unfreezing* or provided a Mezirowian (1991) *disorienting dilemma*. Participatory evaluation and other innovations may be the new habits in Lewin's refreezing phase.

A Role for a Cultural View

How is it helpful in a practical sense for evaluators to frame mainstreaming as a cultural creature? For one, we might listen more carefully to the ways in which organizations and clients talk about evaluation. Instead of simply receiving metaphors as humorous or clever, as I confess I often do, we might use them as a point of serious engagement (Patton, 2000). Is evaluation, for example, a ten-year anniversary? Ammunition? A shield? Colonization? If so, what do these things mean? An early (qualitative) phase of an evaluation, starting with negotiation of the contract, provides opportunities to document important terms. The terms' frequency, their application by different stakeholders, and their connection to choices could inform the evaluator. I am considering adding an "evaluation metaphor" category to my client intake form so that I remember to document in this way.

Second, we might view resistance to new ideas and adherence to old (whatever those might be) less as positivist (or relativist) bull-headedness and more as habits in Lewin's frozen mode. Third, we might relax our expectation that clients and participants in programs readily explain why they prefer or require what seem like outmoded, unhelpful, or unethical evaluation processes. Over time, interpretive forms of evaluation can surface meanings, but if we believe Schön (1983), a coherent explanation is usually not possible at the outset.

If we decide to change evaluation practices that are currently mainstreamed (as participatory evaluators try to do) or attempt to instill a new set of habits (another thing participatory evaluators try to do), we would do well to consider Lewin's unfreezing-freezing model. Such an approach would necessitate an adult education framework that helps clients surface, then unlearn, nonpreferred habits while considering new ones.

Fourth, we might give in to working with the multifaceted, culturally bound purposes of our clients if these purposes enable us to act ethically and effectively. (An evaluator might refuse, for example, to enhance symbolic dimensions of an evaluation that clients talk about as "vengeance.") Evaluators can help clients to consider the implications of aesthetic or symbolic dimensions of the evaluation with regard to scheduling, objectives, data collection, and costs. If, for example, clients say that evaluation must be a *celebration,* it would be prudent to ask how the report might look different from any earlier reports (higher quality? more copies? higher cost?). The presence of authority figures might be more important, and the results might need to be presented at an upcoming event that would ordinarily rush data collection. One might also explore how negative findings would be handled in an evaluation that is intended to be a celebration.

The tacit skill of "psyching out" clients is something that good evaluators already do, at least with the clients with whom they have learned to succeed. Greater attention to cultural and philosophical dimensions of evaluation might help us succeed with different types of clients or help clients face new pressures. What is unworthy of us as social inquirers is to underestimate the complexity of mainstreaming, its tacit control over us as well as over "them." One way to surmount this challenge would be to develop a sense of evaluation as an artifact of culture that evaluators shape rather than originate.

References

Argyris, C., and Schön, D. *Organizational Learning II: Theory, Method, and Practice.* Reading, Mass.: Addison-Wesley, 1996.

Bateson, G. *Mind and Nature: A Necessary Unity.* Toronto: Bantam, 1980.

Chambers, R. *Whose Reality Counts? Putting the First Last.* London: ITP, 1997.

Chelimsky, E., and Shadish, W. R. (eds.). *Evaluation for the Twenty-First Century: A Handbook.* Thousand Oaks, Calif.: Sage, 1997.

Cousins, J. B., and Whitmore, E. "Framing Participatory Evaluation." In E. Whitmore (ed.), *Understanding and Practicing Participatory Evaluation.* New Directions for Evaluation, no. 80. San Francisco: Jossey-Bass, 1998.

Dewey, J. *Logic: The Theory of Inquiry.* New York: Holt, 1938.

Fisher, L., Moeliono, I., and Wodicka, S. "Cattle, Cockatoos, Chameleons, and Ninja Turtles: Seeking Sustainability in Forest Management and Conservation in Nusa Tenggara, Indonesia." Paper presented to the World Bank/Ford/IDRC International

Workshop on Community-Based Natural Resource Management, Washington, D.C., May 1998.

Geertz, C. "Thick Description: Toward an Interpretive Theory of Culture." In C. Geertz (ed.), *The Interpretation of Cultures: Selected Essays.* New York: Basic Books, 1973.

Guba, E. G., and Lincoln, Y. S. *Fourth Generation Evaluation.* Thousand Oaks, Calif.: Sage, 1989.

House, E. R., and Howe, K. R. *Values in Evaluation and Social Research.* Thousand Oaks, Calif.: Sage, 1999.

Joint Committee on Standards for Educational Evaluation. *The Program Evaluation Standards: How to Assess Evaluations of Educational Programs.* (2nd ed.) Thousand Oaks, Calif.: Sage, 1994.

Langsdorf, L., and Smith, A. (eds.). *Recovering Pragmatism's Voice: The Classical Tradition, Rorty, and the Philosophy of Communication.* Albany, N.Y.: SUNY Press, 1995.

Lewin, K. *Resolving Social Conflicts: Selected Papers on Group Dynamics.* New York: HarperCollins, 1948.

Mayer, J. "Environmental Organizing in Indonesia: The Search for a Newer Order." In R. D. Lipschutz (ed.), *Global Civil Society and Global Environmental Governance: The Politics of Nature from Place to Planet.* Albany, N.Y.: SUNY Press, 1996.

Mezirow, J. *Transformative Dimensions of Adult Learning.* San Francisco: Jossey-Bass, 1991.

Patton, M. Q. *Utilization-Focused Evaluation: The New Century Text.* (3rd ed.) Thousand Oaks, Calif.: Sage, 1997.

Patton, M. Q. "Overview: Language Matters." In R. K. Hopson (ed.), *How and Why Language Matters in Evaluation.* New Directions for Evaluation, no. 86. San Francisco, Jossey-Bass, 2000.

Picciotto, R. "The Logic of Mainstreaming: A Development Evaluation Perspective." *Evaluation,* 2002, *8*(3), 322–339.

Rai, K. "Mainstreaming Mendalic Logic Model: Vision and Contradictions." Paper presented at the annual meeting of the American Evaluation Association, St. Louis, Nov. 2001.

Rorty, R. *Consequences of Pragmatism.* Minneapolis: University of Minnesota Press, 1982.

Schön, D. A. *The Reflective Practitioner: How Professionals Think in Action.* New York: Basic Books, 1983.

Wodicka, S. *Report on Workshop to Discuss Preliminary Evaluation Findings on the Impact of the NTCDC 1991–1999.* World Neighbors, South East Asia Regional Office, Ubud, Bali, Indonesia, 1999.

NANCY GRUDENS-SCHUCK is assistant professor of evaluation systems in the Department of Agricultural Education and Studies, Iowa State University, Ames. She is author of the forthcoming book titled, The Mainstream Environmentalist: Learning through Participatory Education (Greenwood Publishing) and is active in the Extension Education Evaluation Topical Interest Group of the AEA.

4

This chapter describes the framework and implementation of a program accountability system in a statewide initiative (South Carolina First Steps to School Readiness), which was developed (1) to enable practitioners to provide evaluation information required by legislative mandate and (2) to develop the capacity of practitioners to systematically plan their program, implement with quality, and self-evaluate. The components of this program are reflected in its name: Planning, Implementation, and Evaluation (PIE). The chapter describes PIE in relation to program theory, usage, and efforts to mainstream.

PIE à la Mode: Mainstreaming Evaluation and Accountability in Each Program in Every County of a Statewide School Readiness Initiative

Abraham Wandersman, Paul Flaspohler, April Ace, Laurie Ford, Pamela S. Imm, Matthew J. Chinman, Jeffrey Sheldon, Arlene Bowers Andrews, Cindy A. Crusto, Joy S. Kaufman

Federal and state legislative requirements increasingly demand evaluation and accountability for treatment, prevention, and education programs (for example, the Government Performance and Results Act of 1993). In addition, funders of nonprofit agencies, such as the United Way and local and national foundations, are requiring specific evaluation plans to measure program outcomes (United Way, 1996). As a result, practitioners such as teachers, preventionists, and health care providers are under increasing pressure to evaluate their efforts and demonstrate outcomes. Yet negative experience or lack of experience with evaluation has led practitioners to resist or marginalize evaluation (Northwest Regional Educational Laboratory, 1999). In these cases, practitioners do not receive potentially valuable evaluation data that can be used to improve and sustain programs.

In this chapter, we describe the framework and implementation of a program accountability system for the initiative, South Carolina First Steps to School Readiness (First Steps). The accountability system was developed to *both* (1) enable practitioners to provide evaluation information required by legislative mandate and (2) develop the capacity of practitioners to systematically plan their program, implement with quality, and self-evaluate. The components of this program are reflected in its name—Planning, Implementation, and Evaluation (PIE)—and they are central to the development, implementation, and evaluation of each program in every county. PIE tools and processes were eventually used to inform program effectiveness reports that were then used to evaluate the first three years of the First Steps initiative.

Model of the Problem

The link between insufficient school readiness and adverse outcomes has received increased attention in recent years. *School readiness* has been defined as a set of capabilities that all children need before entering school. The National Education Goals Panel and the National Association for the Education of Young Children (NAEYC) believe that school readiness needs to recognize individual variation and diversity, inequities in opportunities and access to resources, and the need for appropriate expectations (Kagan, Moore, and Bredekamp, 1995; National Association for the Education of Young Children, 1995).

In order to promote school readiness, many states (for example, North Carolina, California, West Virginia) have developed programs targeting the environmental, physical, and educational factors influencing rates of readiness. South Carolina's statewide initiative was proposed to improve low rates on a variety of indicators of school readiness. A 1999 study revealed that approximately 19 percent of all South Carolina children entering the first grade were "not ready," according to scores on the Cognitive Skills Assessment Battery administered to South Carolina school children. In addition, approximately one-third (33 percent) of South Carolina's kindergartners were rated deficient in Emotional Maturity and Social Confidence; nearly one-half (46 percent) were rated deficient in General Knowledge, and two-thirds (66 percent) were rated deficient in Early Language Skills (Boyer, 1993).

School readiness, as defined by First Steps, encompasses multiple dimensions of learning and development. These dimensions include health and physical development, emotional well-being and social competence, approaches to learning (for example, curiosity, independence, cooperation, and attention), communication skills, cognition, and general knowledge. In order to thoroughly understand the problem of poor school readiness, it was necessary to develop a logic model that reflected the connections among the conditions that contributed to the need for a program, the activities aimed at addressing these conditions, and the outcomes and effects that were expected to result from the activities (Julian, Jones, and Dey, 1995; McEwan and Bigelow, 1997). Goodman and Wandersman (1994) developed a formative evaluation approach called FORECAST that highlights the use of a model of the problem and a model of intervention (or model of the solution). Using this approach, a conceptual model called a "model of the problem" was created to describe the links among all the factors that contribute to the problem of school readiness. In addition, a second model was developed that

Figure 4.1. Model of the Problem: Major Domains of Influence on Child Outcomes

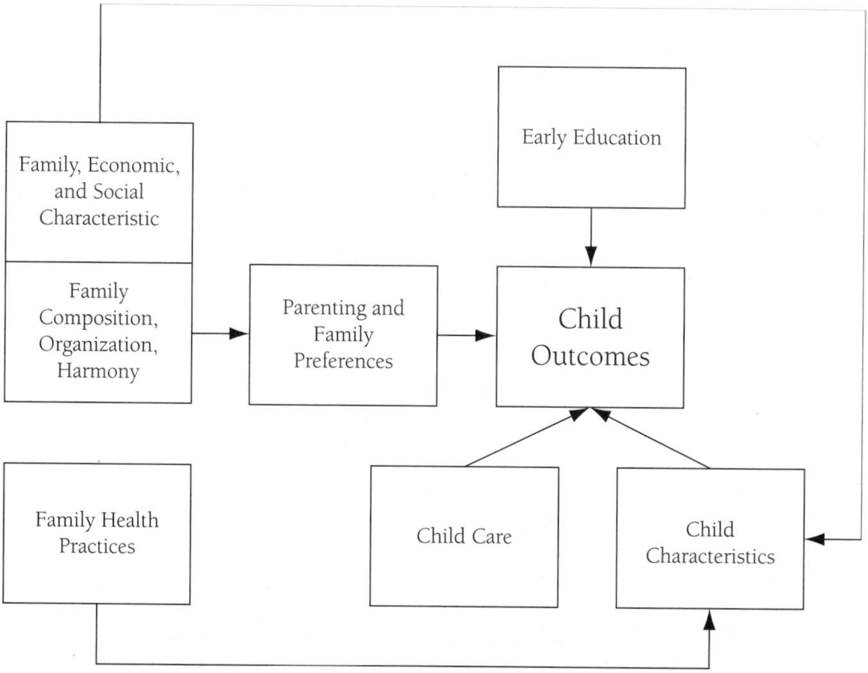

incorporated elements of and logical steps toward a solution. Logical links among various stages and factors form the foundation of these models.

The First Steps model of the problem borrows from an immense birth cohort study (Moore and others, 1999), which is following approximately fifteen thousand children longitudinally from birth through first grade. The study hypothesizes determinants (dimensions) that predict positive and negative child outcomes. The determinants are defined by the First Steps effective practice experts as Early Education, Child Care, Health, Parent Education, Family Strengthening, and Transportation. The South Carolina model of the problem of school readiness used the determinants as predictors of positive and negative child outcomes, which, in turn, predict school readiness (see Figure 4.1).

Model of the Solution

The First Steps initiative was developed to address alarming educational statistics in the state of South Carolina. First Steps is a comprehensive, results-oriented, early childhood education initiative designed to help South Carolina's families ensure that their children reach first grade ready to succeed. The initiative is grounded in the assumption that partnerships among key stakeholders involved with young children within each county will improve school readiness if they consider collaborative strategies to bring about positive changes in the six determinants of school readiness (see Figure 4.2).

The First Steps initiative was created by enabling legislation enacted on June 28, 1999. The legislation outlines the purpose and the process of the initiative. In program theory terms, the legislation provides a model of the solution or a theory of change (Weiss, 1995). The legislation provided funding

Figure 4.2. Model of the Solution: First Steps Grant Implementation Process

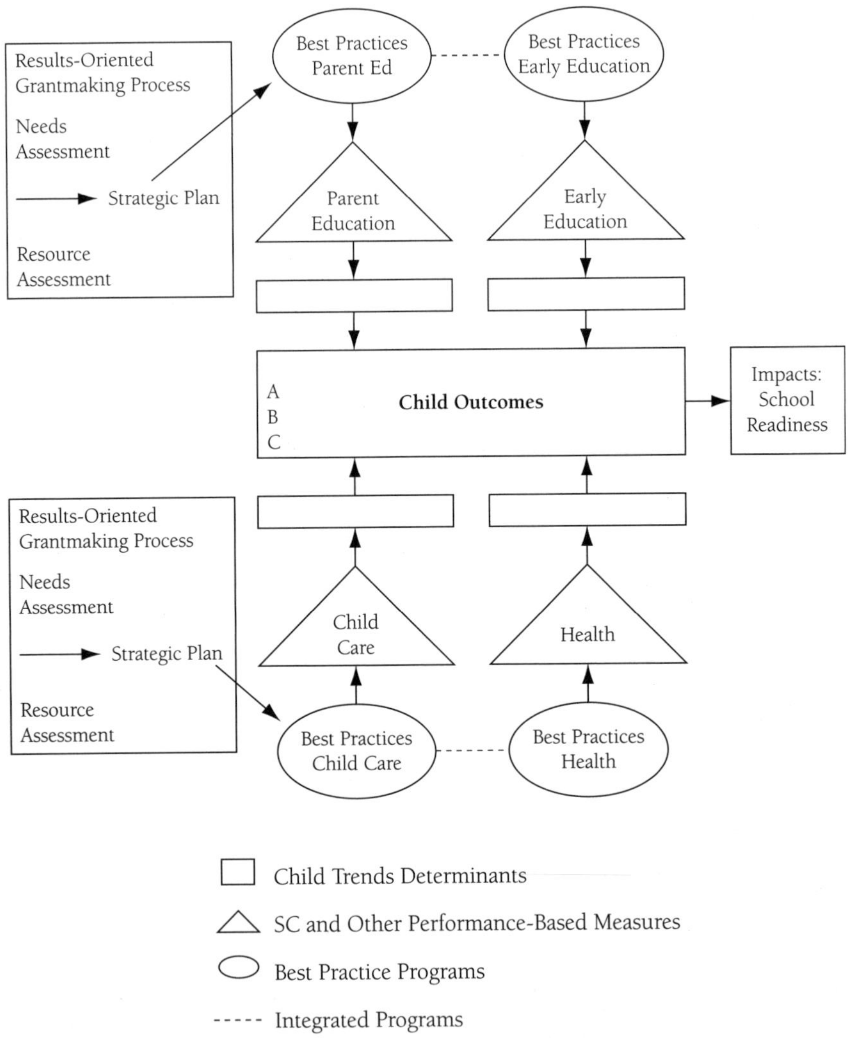

($20 million for the first year and $30 million each year thereafter) and specified how each of the forty-six South Carolina counties could access a portion of that funding: each county would have to form a First Steps county partnership board, composed of local representatives from diverse interest groups and organizations in that county.

The First Steps legislation describes a two-step process by which counties apply for and receive grants for planning and implementing their school readiness strategies. There was an uncanny fit between the legislation and "Getting To Outcomes" strategies for comprehensive quality programming designed to guide self-evaluation (Wandersman, Imm, Chinman, and Kaftarian, 2000). *Getting To Outcomes* (GTO) guides practitioners though the critical steps needed to implement quality programs. The GTO process consists of ten accountability questions, the answers to which serve as a beginning guide to successful planning, implementation, and evaluation of programs. The ten questions are as follows:

1. What are the underlying needs and conditions that need to be addressed?
2. What are the goals, target population, and objectives?
3. What science- or evidence–based models and best practice programs can be useful in reaching the goals?
4. How will the program fit with existing programs already being offered, the organization's mission, and community values?
5. What organizational capacities are needed to implement this program?
6. What is the plan for this program?
7. How will the program be implemented with quality?
8. How well did the program work?
9. How will continuous quality improvement strategies be incorporated?
10. If the program is successful, how will it be sustained?

These ten questions were the basis of the two-step grant application process that met the mandates of the First Steps legislation (see Figure 4.3). The initial phase, Level I, provided counties with resources to develop a collaborative effort, conduct a needs and resource assessment, identify and prioritize gaps, and initiate a strategic planning process geared toward improving school readiness. Upon development of their strategic plans, boards applied for implementation grants in the next phase, Level II. Funding was provided to partnership boards, contingent on the development of high-quality strategies that provided services to improve school readiness. The boards were directed to use science and best practice interventions that would change determinants and produce positive child outcomes. The increase in positive outcomes would consequently support improvements in school readiness. After receiving their Level II funds, counties proceeded to implement their First Steps programs and strategies.

Figure 4.3. Accountability Questions and the First Steps Grant Process

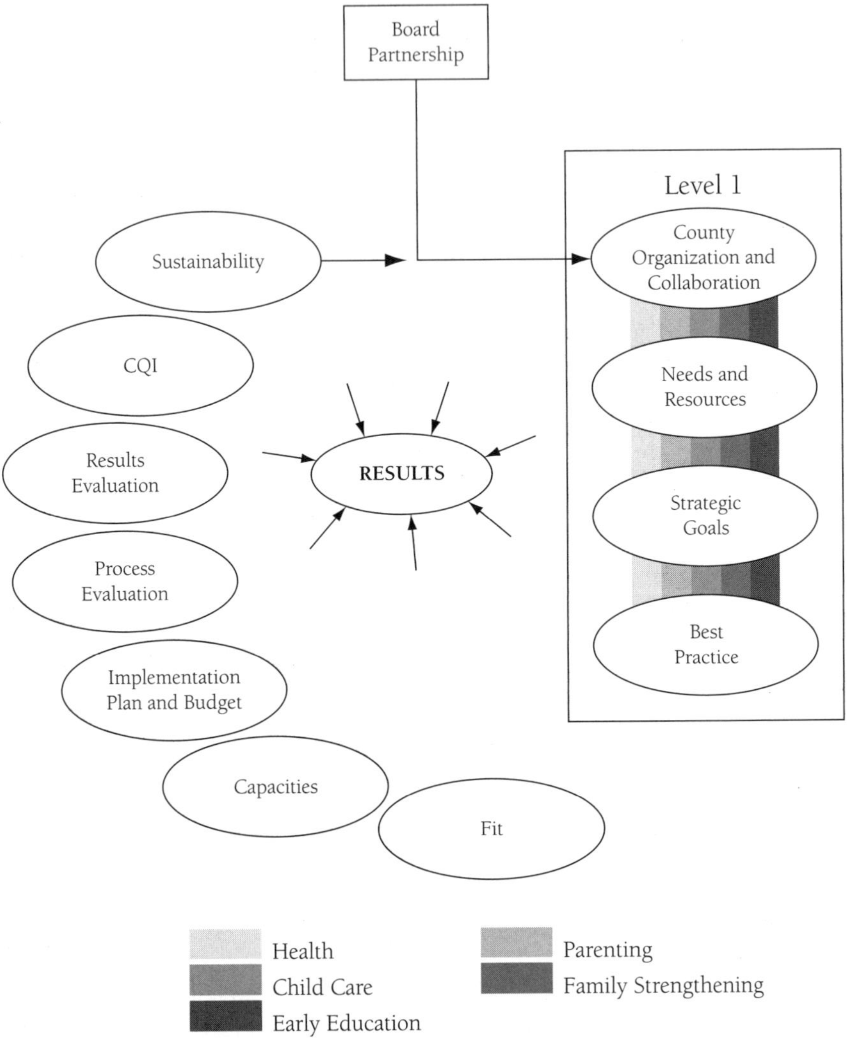

First Steps Evaluation and Accountability

In addition to outlining the formation of county partnership boards and their activities, the First Steps legislation referred directly and indirectly to the accountability and evaluation of programs. For instance, each county partnership board was required to form a collaborative partnership and maximize resources before it received funding for the implementation-management grants. First Steps legislation additionally required the county partnerships to develop internal evaluation procedures to assess partnership functioning, program implementation, progress toward interim goals, client satisfaction, and cost savings attributable to increased efficiency and effectiveness of the new services. These elements, along with recommendations for changes, are required to be reported to the legislature annually over the initial seven years of the initiative. According to section 59–152–160A: "The South Carolina First Steps to School Readiness Board of Trustees shall establish internal evaluation policies and procedures for County First Steps Partnerships for an annual review of the functioning of the partnership, implementation of strategies, and progress made toward the interim goals and benchmarks."

Further, Section 59–152–70 indicates that the partnership boards must collect information and submit annual reports to the First Steps board of trustees. The requirements of the annual report were clearly delineated in the legislation. The legislation required that the county board submit an annual report that includes (but is not limited to) information regarding

- The current level and effectiveness of services for children and families
- Strategic goals
- Monitoring of progress toward strategic goals
- Report on implementation of activities
- Recommendations for changes to the strategic plan
- Evaluation and report of program effectiveness and client satisfaction before, during, and after the implementation of the strategic plan
- Estimation of cost savings attributable to increased efficiency

The priority of results and accountability in the legislation was clear. The legislative intent and requirements were consistent with theory and practice in community development (Fawcett and others, 1995), empowerment evaluation (Fetterman, Kaftarian, and Wandersman, 1996), evaluation of health and human service programs in community settings (Telfair, Leviton, and Merchant, 1999), and results-oriented grantmaking (Yost and Wandersman, 1998) for effective programs. These literatures suggest that building the evaluation capacity of practitioners to incorporate approaches and tools of evaluation into programming leads to more effective programs.

> The goal of empowerment evaluation is to improve program success. By providing program developers with understanding and tools for assessing the planning, implementation, and results of programs, program personnel have the opportunity to improve planning and implementation of programs and thereby increase the probability of achieving results [Wandersman, 1999, p. 96].

It was anticipated that counties would benefit from a standardized, yet adaptable, system to assist them in systematically collecting, organizing, and reporting data and program information necessary for planning and implementing programs.

The PIE System. A comprehensive program accountability system was needed to guide the county partnerships in planning and implementing their programs by helping them collect, organize, evaluate, use, and report this information and results for program improvement and accountability purposes. Most important, a practitioner-friendly approach was required, as each county would have significant responsibility for conducting evaluation activities, and funding for professional external evaluators was limited. The PIE system builds on approaches and tools consistent with participatory (Cousins and Earl, 1992; Mathison, 1994) and empowerment evaluation (Fetterman, Kaftarian, and Wandersman, 1996).

PIE helped all forty-six counties participating in First Steps do the following:

- Plan a variety of school readiness programs across the six areas outlined in the legislation
- Implement these programs with high quality
- Conduct their own evaluations with support from personnel, called PIE consultants, hired by the Office of First Steps to support the county boards

Tools and processes for PIE were developed in collaboration with a network of local effective practice experts in each of the determinant areas of intervention targeted by First Steps. This effective practice network (EPN) was an integral part of the PIE process—editing and approving evaluation plans and providing advice and guidance on an ongoing basis. An overarching purpose of the introduction of PIE into the First Steps process was to standardize assessment and evaluation tools across the state of South Carolina. In this way, data could be aggregated and compared easily. Central features of the PIE system are the PIE shell, the PIE workbook, and the *PIE Trainer's Manual,* which is used in consultation with a PIE consultant.

PIE Components. Major bases of ideas for tools in PIE were manuals titled *Prevention Plus III* (Linney and Wandersman, 1991) and *Getting To Outcomes* (Wandersman, Imm, Chinman, and Kaftarian, 2000). These manuals use an empowerment evaluation approach and contain tools for planning, process, outcome, and impact-evaluation for substance abuse prevention programs. The approaches were developed to teach people at the local level the basics about planning and implementation and conducting elementary evaluations of their own programs. PIE uses the latest iteration of these materials to stimulate analytical thinking about the ways programs might produce outcomes, realistic thinking about the possible effects of any program, and careful planning for the implementation of any program.

PIE Shell. In contemporary usage, PIE "a la mode" is interpreted as a piece of pie with ice cream on top. The literal translation of the French *à la mode* is "in the style" or "in the fashion." This translation is in keeping with the customizable nature of the PIE components and PIE process. The PIE shell was designed to be flexible and comprehensive enough to account for the variation in the school readiness programming that was to be present across all forty-six counties during Level II, yet it was also designed with a degree of standardization that allows for aggregate reporting across the entire state, within-state comparisons, and linkages to the external evaluation required by the First Steps legislation. In brief, PIE shells are standardized and customizable.

The PIE shell is a worksheet that provides a format for guiding program staff through and documenting each step of the three-step (planning, implementation, and evaluation) process. The planning step was designed to assist the partnership boards or program personnel in articulating several aspects of their approach to improving school readiness. Specifically, the planning section of the PIE shell prompted users to identify and describe the goals and purposes, target population, objectives, collaboration partners, activities, integration efforts, outputs, budget, and cost savings. The planning section assisted counties in meeting the legislative requirement of documenting strategic goals. This section also laid the groundwork for other legislative requirements.

In the implementation step of the PIE shell, practitioners kept a running record of progress, problems, and lessons learned for each of the elements recorded during planning. Practitioners could document the extent to which they achieved elements of their plan. This information could also be used as an impetus for altering aspects of a program in order to improve the likelihood of achieving results. By monitoring activities and progress related to the program plan, programs fulfilled legislative requirements for monitoring the level and effectiveness of services for children and families, monitoring progress toward strategic goals, and producing a report on implementation of activities.

The evaluation section mirrored the implementation section but allowed for interim and final summation of progress gleaned from the implementation section of PIE. Completing the evaluation section assisted the counties in meeting the legislative mandates regarding cost-effectiveness and cost savings, as well as reporting progress toward their stated goals.

The PIE shell fulfilled three basic needs of a program accountability system for First Steps:

1. Program Level: Provided structure and tools necessary to facilitate data collection, analysis, and local feedback for a broad range of program types
2. County Level: Provided the county board with a system for evaluating how well different types of programs were influencing school readiness within a county
3. State Level: Provided a system for developing a knowledge base regarding best practices in promoting school readiness and answering

state-level questions about the effectiveness of interventions in different determinant domains

PIE Workbook. The PIE workbook provided basic instructions for using the PIE system and examples of PIE shells that had already been completed for a variety of school readiness programs the counties were likely to implement. Therefore, counties have an example to follow when considering the implementation of programs that have already been "shelled." In addition to the basic instructions and completed PIE shells, the workbook included an introduction to program evaluation and information about science and best practice standards for effective programs. The PIE workbook was designed to be expandable, allowing for inclusion of new PIE shells as they were being developed for different county programs. Counties considering the implementation of programs that had already been shelled benefited from information in the completed shells when developing PIE shells for their own program.

PIE Trainer's Manual. The *PIE Trainer's Manual* was designed to assist PIE consultants working directly with each county partnership board and their programs and other key First Steps personnel with the PIE process. The manual describes the activities and steps to follow when consulting with board members or practitioners. These steps ranged from precontact background research to initial visits to completion of PIE shells.

PIE Process. Using the general framework of PIE and the *PIE Trainer's Manual*, the PIE team of consultants worked closely with members of each county partnership board, county First Steps staff (executive director and assistants), and staff from specific programs to ensure that the PIE process was introduced and worksheets customized to best promote accountability. The consultation process and implementation of the PIE system varied considerably according to a county's grant application status, that is, when they received their funding and were allowed to proceed with the implementation of their programs. PIE consultants and effective practice experts worked together to ensure that customized PIE shells fit with knowledge regarding best practice.

PIE Consultants. PIE consultants were the frontline workers of the PIE process. Employed by the Office of First Steps through a contract with the Institute for Families in Society at the University of South Carolina, PIE consultants provided training in collaboration with the county partnership boards, county First Steps staff, and program practitioners. Each county had a PIE consultant assigned to it with the two full-time consultants working in ten counties each and the remaining half-time consultants working across the rest of the state.

Effective Practice Network. Content experts in each of the dimensions of school readiness provided a deeper knowledge base from which to draw when tailoring PIE shells to the needs of individual counties. These experts were retained by the Office of First Steps for consultation directly with the counties through the PIE consultants. Members of the EPN were tapped previously by First Steps to develop papers on effective practice to assist in the development of county strategic First Steps plans. The operation of the PIE system required that the program staff and county board members provide data to the Office of First Steps and that PIE consultants and members of the EPN would provide a great deal of personalized technical assistance.

PIE and County Stages of Development

At full scale, we expected that there would be approximately four hundred programs operating each year with funding from First Steps. As is often the case with initiatives of this scope, the programs began running before sufficient resources and preparation were put in place in order to bring the project to scale. As a result, PIE was introduced to county boards in two distinct stages of development: (1) Level II Approved Counties and (2) Counties Preparing Level II Applications. Just as the First Steps initiative was mandated for political reasons to go to scale sooner than it was ready, so too was the PIE system.

Level II Approved Counties. PIE shells were customized to meet specific requirements for each program or strategy. With county partnerships that had already received Level II funding, a PIE consultant met with county representatives to (1) provide an overview of the general accountability concepts behind PIE to the county partnership members and program staff, (2) gather more specific details about the proposed programming (for example, more specifics than may be present in the Level II grant application document), and (3) collaboratively develop a system within the general PIE framework to facilitate the planning, implementation, and evaluation of their programs. The initial entrée of the PIE consultant was made into a county through the Office of First Steps technical assistant assigned to that county. The PIE consultants were in constant and ongoing communication with county partnership board members, county First Steps staff, or specific program staff throughout the PIE process. In an empowerment evaluation framework, the success of program personnel in adopting and implementing a PIE type of system requires ongoing coaching and mentoring, as well as guidance and motivation from the evaluation coach—in this case, the PIE consultant.

Counties Preparing Level II Applications. PIE was designed to be part of the strategic planning process from the beginning to ensure that evaluation was built into the plan for each program or strategy in every county. When counties completed their needs and resource assessments and were in the process of identifying gaps in service needs and developing a strategic plan, the PIE framework helped the counties develop strategic plans and Level II applications that met legislative requirements for approval. PIE consultants worked with counties in the process of strategic planning (1) to provide an overview of the general accountability concepts behind PIE to the county partnership board members, county First Steps staff, and program staff, and (2) to collaboratively develop a strategic plan for school readiness initiatives within the general PIE framework.

Because all of the counties were using the same First Steps PIE system (PIE documents, PIE consultants), the data collected from the programs in each of the partnerships could be aggregated for statewide reporting and within-state comparisons. In addition, the data collected could be linked to the external outcome evaluation so that the effectiveness of different services and dosages could be examined in relation to the final outcomes of school readiness.

Counties Using PIE to Fulfill Reporting Requirements. Although PIE was designed and used to guide nonevaluators through a program accountability process, its utility and flexibility were manifested when counties were asked to produce program effectiveness reports (PERs) as part of the statewide external evaluation of First Steps. At the beginning of 2003, an evaluation report was due to the South Carolina General Assembly; in part, this report was to be produced with information gathered in the PERs. With the advent of the PERs, the PIE consultants' attention was immediately directed away from the PIE process, and they were given less than six months to help counties produce a report for each First Steps funded program. When the 100-item, ten-page PER template was introduced to the counties, their immediate response, predictably, was one of shock. This new requirement posed a daunting, unexpected, and unwelcome task for counties that had limited resources in time and personnel. Concerns were allayed when the PIE consultants showed counties that many of the items could be addressed through information they already had in their PIE documents, especially the information contained in the P and I sections. Unfortunately, some counties received Level II allocations in the later rounds of First Steps funding; these counties did not benefit from thorough PIE consultations because of the unexpected move to PERs and thus had to generate data they did not already have.

How PIE Overcomes Common Barriers to Evaluation

The term *mainstreaming* is used frequently in education, referring to the education of students with disabilities in the same environments as people without disabilities. The process of integrating marginalized students with disability into the general population of a school was initiated largely through legislative mandate (for example, the Individuals with Disabilities Education Act amendments of 1997) and was greeted with resistance. *Mainstreaming*, then, refers to making something (students or evaluation) an integral part of the daily professional responsibilities of an organization. Mainstreaming evaluation means making it a central part of good programming, as opposed to a marginalized activity. In his presidential address to the

AEA, Sanders (2001) defined mainstreaming evaluation as "the process of evaluation activities becoming an integral part of the everyday operations of an organization" (p. 1). He distinguished among *capacity building* (improving the quality of evaluation and its use), *institutionalizing evaluation* (committing formally to evaluation in policy and procedures), and *mainstreaming evaluation* (internalizing and acting on evaluation as a value).

Evaluation as a core organizational value is wholly consistent with our stated practice and philosophy of empowerment evaluation (see Wandersman and others, forthcoming). The principles of empowerment evaluation propose that building capacity and institutionalizing evaluation are some of the key ingredients of empowerment evaluation. In the case of First Steps, evaluation was institutionalized from the start in the language of the legislation and in early commitment to develop suitable tools and processes for evaluation. As stated previously, capacity building was a primary responsibility of the evaluation consultants. In addition to building technical skills required to self-evaluate, a key consideration in PIE processes involved reducing fears about evaluation on the part of program participants and other key stakeholders. The term and concept of mainstreaming captures well the aims and purposes of empowerment evaluation and the PIE system.

As with mainstreaming in education, mainstreaming in evaluation is likely to be met with resistance and fear. According to the Northwest Regional Educational Laboratory (1999), some common complaints and fears about program evaluation are

- Evaluation creates anxiety among program staff.
- Staff may be unsure about how to conduct evaluation.
- Evaluation can interfere with good program activities or compete with services for scarce resources.
- Evaluation results can be misused and misinterpreted, especially by program opponents.

Next, we discuss ways that PIE was designed to address four barriers to mainstreaming evaluation: (1) anxiety, (2) uncertainty, (3) costs, and (4) misuse.

Anxiety. PIE attempted to ease practitioners' anxieties about evaluation by providing them with an effective program accountability system and by empowering individuals with the tools and responsibility for program evaluation. The PIE process, by framing evaluation as part of good programming and training practitioners in evaluation techniques, attempted to move the process of evaluation from the margins into the mainstream. The empowerment evaluation approach decreased anxiety associated with evaluation by placing considerable control for evaluation in the hands of the practitioner.

It has been the experience of PIE consultants that the typical practitioner's initial resistance is based on undernourished evaluation capacity.

When confronted with the prospect of evaluating a program, the practitioner attempts to evaluate the whole thing at once rather than break a program into various components. PIE consultants worked with practitioners to systematically deconstruct a program into critical elements that can be evaluated. Breaking programs down into their smaller, measurable parts reduced practitioners' fears.

Uncertainty. In terms of uncertainty about how to conduct an evaluation, the response to the PIE system and PIE process was very positive. One PIE consultant reported: "I have found in nearly all cases that program folks already *know* how to evaluate their program, they just don't know that they know until I asked questions, prompted by the PIE shell, that were a little more in depth. . . . Once they really looked at what they were doing. . . . they were able to figure out. . . . what to measure, why it needs to be measured, and how to measure it." PIE provided systematic structure and ongoing technical assistance to guide practitioners through the evaluation process. Some county board members, who represent other agencies or organizations, carried the principles of program accountability to their own programs as a result of exposure to PIE.

Costs. Although evaluation costs may compete with the cost of services, we take the stance that they are not separate from programming costs. The costs associated with PIE are actually costs that are part of good programming. First Steps legislation required that counties provide information regarding cost avoidance associated with each program. *Cost avoidance* refers to the reduction in future expenditures that can be attributed to the direct results of an initiative (for example, the cost of incarceration for every juvenile for whom incarceration was prevented). Cost avoidance cannot be calculated without measuring the extent to which a program has achieved its stated goals. Money spent for this type of evaluation can lead to future savings, as less funding may be wasted on inefficient or ineffective programs.

Misuse. Because the local practitioners will be directly involved in all aspects of the evaluation process, they will be in a better position to prevent evaluation information from being misused or unused. For instance, they will have an intimate knowledge of all the evaluation information that is generated from the program by using the PIE framework and, as a result, will be able to respond appropriately to critiques of the program with systematic and objective information. In addition, PIE provided a process for self-correction and, though no program accountability system can guarantee results, using the results-based PIE process increases the probability of achieving results.

Conclusion

Organizational cultures exert influence on practitioners' concerns about anxiety, uncertainty, costs, and misuse. In addition to the need to assist practitioners in overcoming their fears and complaints about evaluation, effective mainstreaming of evaluation can only be achieved within an organizational structure that embraces evaluation. By making evaluation a part of the total process of planning, implementing, and evaluating programs with quality, we are infusing evaluation-friendly traits into the institutional culture of First Steps. Bringing together representatives from a mixture of agencies and interests promoted increased cross-talk among practitioners as part of the process of customizing PIE shells. As a result, the PIE process promoted sharing information and resources.

In sum, PIE was a central part of the First Steps program process and represented a systematic effort to make evaluation a standard practice of good programming. The PIE system was used in planning, implementing, evaluating, and reporting. PIE was used to promote accountability at the program level, the county level, and state level. It helped the State Office of First Steps and county boards to fulfill their responsibilities to the legislature, according to the First Steps strategic plan. We see PIE in First Steps as PIE à la mode (shaped to fulfill many of the requirements for accountability), not as PIE in the sky.

References

Boyer, E. L. "Ready to Learn: A Mandate for the Nation." *Young Children,* 1993, *48,* 54–57.

Cousins, J. B., and Earl, L. M. "The Case for Participatory Evaluation." *Educational Evaluation and Policy Analysis,* 1992, *14,* 397–418.

Fawcett, S. B., and others. "Using Empowerment Theory in Collaborative Partnerships for Community Health and Development." *American Journal of Community Psychology,* 1995, 22, 471–496.

Fetterman, D., Kaftarian, S., and Wandersman, A. (eds.). *Empowerment Evaluation: Knowledge and Tools for Self-Assessment and Accountability.* Thousand Oaks, Calif.: Sage, 1996.

Goodman, R. M., and Wandersman, A. "FORECAST: A Formative Approach to Evaluating Community Coalitions and Community-Based Initiatives." In S. Kaftarian and W. Hansen (eds.), *Journal of Community Psychology Monograph Series,* Center for Substance Abuse Prevention, Special Issue, 1994.

Julian, J. A., Jones, A., and Dey, D. "Open Systems Evaluation and the Logic Model: Program Planning and Evaluation Tools." *Evaluation and Program Planning,* 1995, *18,* 333–341.

Kagan, S. L., Moore, E., and Bredekamp, S. *Reconsidering Children's Early Development and Learning: Toward Common Views and Vocabulary.* Washington, D.C.: National Education Goals Panel, 1995.

Linney, J. A., and Wandersman, A. *Prevention Plus III: Assessing Alcohol and other Drug Prevention Programs at the School and Community Level: A Four-Step Guide to Useful Program Assessment.* Rockville, Md.: U.S. Department of Health and Human Services, Office for Substance Abuse Prevention, 1991.

Mathison, S. "Rethinking the Evaluator Role: Partnership Between Organizations and Evaluators." *Evaluation and Program Planning,* 1994, *17,* 299–304.

McEwan, K. L., and Bigelow, D. A. "Using a Logic Model to Focus Health Services on Population Health Goals." *Canadian Journal of Program Evaluation,* 1997, *12,* 167–174.

Moore, K., and others. *A Birth Cohort Study: Conceptual and Design Considerations and Rationale.* Washington, D.C.: U.S. Department of Education: Office of Educational Research and Improvement, Jan. 1999.

National Association for the Education of Young Children. *School Readiness: A Position Statement of the National Association for the Education of Young Children.* Washington, D.C.: National Association for the Education of Young Children, 1995.

Northwest Regional Educational Laboratory (National Mentoring Center). *Making the Case: Measuring the Impact of Your Mentoring Program.* Portland, Ore.: Northwest Regional Laboratory, 1999. [http://www.nwrel.org/mentoring/pdf/makingcase.pdf].

Sanders, J. "On Mainstreaming Evaluation: Presidential Address." Paper presented at the sixteenth annual conference of the American Evaluation Association, St. Louis, Nov. 2001.

South Carolina. First Steps to School Readiness Act, Title 59, Chap. 152, 1999.

Telfair, J., Leviton, L. C., and Merchant, J. S. (eds.). *Evaluating Health and Human Service Programs in Community Settings.* New Directions for Evaluation, no. 93. San Francisco: Jossey-Bass, 1999.

United Way of America. *Measuring Program Outcomes: A Practical Approach.* Alexandria, Va.: United Way of America, 1996.

Wandersman, A. (ed.). *Framing the Evaluation of Health and Human Service Programs in Community Settings: Assessing Progress.* New Directions for Evaluation, no. 83. San Francisco: Jossey-Bass, 1999.

Wandersman, A., Imm, P., Chinman, M., and Kaftarian, S. "Getting to Outcomes: A Results-Based Approach to Accountability." *Evaluation and Program Planning,* 2000, *23,* 389–395.

Wandersman, A., and others. "Empowerment Evaluation: Principles and Action." In L. A. Jason and others (eds.), *Participatory Community Research: Theories and Methods in Action.* American Psychological Association: Washington, D.C., forthcoming.

Wandersman, A., and others. "Comprehensive Quality Programming and Accountability: Eight Essential Strategies for Implementing Successful Prevention Programs." *Journal of Primary Prevention,* 1998, *19,* 3–30.

Weiss, C. H. "Nothing as Practical as Good Theory: Exploring Theory-Based Evaluation for Comprehensive Community Initiatives for Children and Families." In J. P. Connell, A. Kubisch, L. Schorr, and C. H. Weiss (eds.), *New Approaches to Evaluating Community Initiatives: Concepts, Methods, and Contexts.* Washington, D.C.: Aspen Institute, 1995.

Yost, J., and Wandersman, A. "Results-Oriented Grant-Making/Grant-Implementation: Mary Black Foundation's Experience." Paper presented at the American Evaluation Association conference, St. Louis, 1998.

ABRAHAM WANDERSMAN is professor of psychology at the University of South Carolina, He won the Myrdal Award for Evaluation Practice in 1998 from the American Evaluation Association.

PAUL FLASPOHLER is a predoctoral fellow at Yale University School of Medicine. He is completing the doctorate in clinical-community psychology at the University of South Carolina.

APRIL ACE is an attorney and doctoral candidate in clinical-community psychology at the University of South Carolina. She will be employed at the James A. Haley VA Hospital in Tampa, Florida, for a one-year clinical psychology internship.

LAURIE FORD is an associate professor of education and counseling psychology and special education at the University of British Columbia, focusing on family and community factors that promote school readiness and the family-school partnership.

PAMELA S. IMM is a community psychologist in Syracuse, New York. She is director of research and evaluation at Action Research Associates, a nonprofit organization specializing in empowerment evaluation, community consultation, and action research.

MATTHEW J. CHINMAN is an associate behavioral scientist at the RAND Corporation and health science specialist at the West Los Angeles VA Mental Illness Research, Education, and Clinical Center.

JEFFREY SHELDON is a research associate in the Department of Psychology at the University of South Carolina and works as a program evaluator with community coalitions and programs.

ARLENE BOWERS ANDREWS is a professor of social work and the director and cofounder of the Institute for Families in Society at the University of South Carolina, where she specializes in public-private sector collaboration and family policy.

CINDY A. CRUSTO is an instructor in the Division of Prevention and Community Research, Department of Psychiatry, Yale School of Medicine. She also serves as associate director of program and service system evaluation at the Consultation Center in New Haven, Connecticut.

JOY S. KAUFMAN is an assistant professor of psychology in psychiatry at the Yale University School of Medicine. She directs the program and service system evaluation area of the Consultation Center in New Haven, Connecticut, and codirects the evaluation research area of the Division of Prevention and Community Research at Yale.

5

Approaches to training in evaluation, with the aim of seeding the field of education with evaluators who can work with organizations in a more participatory and relevant way, are proposed. The methods suggested are intended to incline evaluators toward participatory approaches. Trained evaluators will be equipped to forge powerful learning partnerships with programs and participants, thus improving the prospects for mainstreaming evaluation.

Helping Evaluators Swim with the Current: Training Evaluators to Support Mainstreaming

J. Jackson Barnette, Anne Baber Wallis

In his introduction to this volume, Sanders exhorts university faculty to "take the lead in preparing evaluators for leadership roles in organizations, or in preparing leaders for evaluation roles in organizations" as a means of promoting the mainstreaming of evaluation. On the face of it, his main objective is to train more evaluators, who will then be available to provide full-time or consultation support to organizations. Evaluators will thus be available to colonize organizations with needed evaluation support; we hope the result will be progress toward mainstreamed evaluation.

We agree that training in the areas of psychology, social work, public health, medicine, nursing, education, public administration, and related fields could benefit from access to educational offerings in evaluation research. However, we contend that it is not just the availability of these offerings but their content and quality that will determine whether or not evaluation is broadly accepted as a fundamental feature in these types of organizations so that mainstreaming evaluation is facilitated.

In this chapter, we propose approaches to training in evaluation, both within and outside the formal educational setting, that aim to seed the field with evaluators who are able to work with organizations in a manner that is overtly participatory and relevant. We suggest ways to grow evaluators with a value set that inclines them toward participatory approaches, skills that support the integrated development of logic models and theories of change in consort with program staff, and a pragmatic approach toward evaluation that encourages the development of useful and realistic outcome setting. We suggest that better-trained, more participatory, more pragmatic evaluators will be equipped to forge powerful learning partnerships with programs and participants. These new evaluators will pave the way for better-integrated evaluations, the transfer of basic evaluation methods to communities, and an improved prospect for mainstreaming evaluation. We recommend and describe innovative training techniques in consort with a system that integrates practical traineeships, graduate-level mentorships, postgraduate fellowships, and awards for innovative approaches that support mainstreaming.

What's Wrong (and Sometimes Right) About Our Usual Way of Doing Business

In our work, we have often met program staff of community-based organizations, local and state government agencies, schools and universities, and medical and health care organizations who have never worked with an evaluator in a participatory manner. We have heard stories about evaluators who "worked with" a project for years but never once encountered a participant, attended a program activity, or met with line staff. We have heard about evaluators who did not work to fully understand an intervention or struggle with staff to outline goals and objectives or articulate a theory of change. Too often, researchers "do evaluation to" programs or "evaluate against" program objectives that were written into a grant application and do not necessarily reflect the organic reality of most programs or organizations. In these evaluations, the researcher has placed herself well outside the boundaries of the program, often with the perfectly respectable goal of maintaining objectivity. This evaluator was, no doubt, schooled in the traditional textbook-perfect research methods taught in one of the many excellent graduate programs offered in the United States and elsewhere. One unfortunate and unexpected result is that our textbook-grounded evaluator may sacrifice validity because she has not been involved enough to fully understand the program, has not taken into account ways in which the program has digressed from its protocol (no doubt out of necessity, not out of naiveté), and has not factored in the many logistical and human challenges that most staff and participants face in social, educational, and health services environments. Finally, her "outsider" attitude may have unintentionally alienated program staff and community members and perpetuated an entrenched view of evaluator and program staff as, if not actually adversarial, individuals with very different and unrelated roles and agendas.

We suggest that working closely with program staff and participants is not only a healthy (and accepted) way of doing evaluation research but one that moves programs toward a real acceptance of how they can use evaluation theory and methods to better their programs and learn from their experiences. The idea that this approach is important and that it requires a seismic paradigm shift is not a new one. Nina Wallerstein (1999, 2000), David Fetterman, Abraham Wandersman, and many others (for example, Fetterman, 2001; Fetterman, Shakeh, Kaftarian, and Wandersman, 1996) have done an outstanding job of articulating the need to conduct less power-sensitive, more participatory approaches to evaluation.

The remaining question is how to integrate this approach at multiple levels into the academic curriculum and current practice so that we *tell* our students how to do evaluation in a more inclusive way, *show* them how to do it, and then *guide* them as they begin to practice what they have learned.

Finally, we accept the idea that mainstreaming evaluation is a good thing, especially to the extent that programs accept the need for evaluation and conduct certain evaluative activities on a routine basis. However, we have a caveat: we assert that mainstreaming evaluation need not necessarily mean that all aspects of evaluation be conducted by a program with no outside guidance. Good evaluation research is hard to do. Sometimes in our efforts to empower programs, we imply that evaluation can be a do-it-yourself job. At a most basic level, self-evaluation could introduce significant bias due to lack of objectivity. However, bias would also be introduced when methods are improperly selected, poor or untested surveys are employed in an inappropriate way to measure change, or analytical methods are improperly applied. In short, a little knowledge can be dangerous. Sanders aptly notes in this issue that "poor evaluation can be worse than no evaluation at all for an organization."

Mainstreaming evaluation should mean that education, health, and social service organizations incorporate concepts of evaluation into their planning and thinking, that they include an evaluation (preferably with support from an outside evaluation consultant) from the inception of their program, and that they understand the fundamental ways that evaluation can be used to improve how they think about their program and its intended (and possibly actual) outcomes.

Who Needs Training in Evaluation for Mainstreaming?

This may sound like a ridiculous question, but we need to consider it. There are two obvious responses at the outset: (1) everyone and (2) a select few. Both responses are valid, and both reflect current thinking in the field about mainstreaming.

In reality, for mainstreaming of evaluation to occur, evaluation training must be a constant and it should permeate all levels of an organization. Therefore, we should train everyone. Of course, levels and modes of evaluation training will vary considerably, depending on needs, existing skill base, type of organization, and so on. Training everyone accepts the premise that if we are to realize the promise of mainstreamed evaluation, everyone must have some basic knowledge and appreciation of evaluation.

We already have programs in place to teach evaluation skills for the select few who intend to conduct or manage evaluations, but that does not fully meet the need because these are not the only groups with a claim or responsibility to participate in or conduct evaluation. If we were not concerned about mainstreaming evaluation, perhaps these two groups could function to provide what on the surface might seem to be evaluation with face validity: it looks good, but there is no evidence that it *is* good. In virtually every discipline, coursework should include topics in evaluation as core concepts. It should become second nature to expect evaluation to be a part of all coursework and real-world practice. Informal evaluation is always taking place, but we know how biased that can be. To positively influence the use of sound evaluation practices, efforts must be made to mainstream it into training as well as into practice. Formal training in evaluation is typically conducted as in-service training with workshops and special on-the-job training or as graduate-level training. Duignan (this issue) has provided a thorough description of in-service training that includes the following: brief presentations; two-day Level I courses; more advanced two-day Level II courses; one-week workshops for policymakers, funders, service providers, and researchers; workshops for managers; one-day overview workshops for managers and service providers, and one-day workshops for staff and management.

Let's return to the "select few." This chapter concentrates on the formal graduate-level training of future evaluators, as well as those who will be assigned the task of managing evaluations. Who should these trainees be?

In the thirty-five to forty years that formal evaluation training has been in existence, training has consisted mostly of the traditional educational and social science research methods, with perhaps a little more emphasis on field-based work. Heavy doses of research methods, statistical analysis, and survey research were administered to about anyone who had the inclination to be an evaluator. Since the early sixties, formal courses and degree or certification programs in evaluation have expanded. The majority of these programs have included the remnants of the early classical methodological focus; however, many programs have moved toward provision of other types of skills and competencies such as modeling, triangulation, systems theory, social and behavioral determinants, and interpersonal skills. Clearly, the field has evolved in very positive ways that reflect mainstreaming as a tacit (if not explicit) goal.

We believe that with these new skill and competency areas comes a need to reassess who should be trained in evaluation. Should we be more selective? Should we look for certain traits or characteristics? Do we try to attract people with the interests and capabilities to conduct and promote mainstreamed evaluation? We're not at all sure we do. We suggest that there is a need to assess the skills and dispositions of those who are interested in being evaluators in relation to skills and dispositions needed to conduct and promote mainstreamed evaluation. Although it is beyond the scope of this chapter to take a definitive look at this need, it is clearly one that the field needs to consider soon. Some skills and dispositions would seem obvious, such as flexibility, ability to communicate (listen and respond), skill in analyzing and problem solving, a nonthreatening demeanor, and so on. Those attributes need to be identified, and we need to be more proactive about getting individuals into evaluation careers who can do more than apply the methods. In the remainder of this chapter, we concentrate on the formal graduate-level training of evaluation professionals.

How Do We Incorporate Evaluation in Graduate Training?

Most evaluation textbooks are rather dry affairs, the best of which incorporate interesting and relevant case examples into the didactic material; others seem to perpetuate tired images of evaluator-as-bureaucrat or wrong ideas about auditing programs. Better examples of evaluation training clearly occur in the classroom, where the personality and experiences of instructors can be used to exorcise the spirit of dull texts and encourage students to think more creatively about evaluation methodology.

Practical experiences can augment classroom teaching, giving students the opportunity to work in an apprenticeship capacity, where they can learn directly about problem solving and relationship building with stakeholders. Certainly, graduate students must learn the fundamentals of research and evaluation methods, but having done so, they should be given the opportunity to break the rules they have learned when it is appropriate and to solve problems in an active and creative way. In other words, after they learn to play the classical violin, they should try to play a little jazz.

We offer two main ingredients for inclusion in the evaluation research curriculum as one component of a multifaceted training experience for students and new professionals: (1) using theory in learning and (2) encouraging the use of live, hands-on experiences. The overarching goal is to promote the mainstreaming of evaluation and evaluative thinking in education, social, and health programs.

First, we recommend including theory as an active learning tool; in this case, we mean teaching how to construct theories of change that can steer programs and evaluation. Successful approaches to adult learning usually integrate traditional didactic methods with the opportunity for hands-on experiences offered through classroom discussion, role-playing, and assignments (Lowman, 1995). Throughout the discussion that follows, we have sprinkled examples for integrating each topic into the curriculum, based on our experiences that include using case studies and "live" learning exercises that exploit opportunities to hear directly from program staff about their experiences with evaluation and their suggestions for improving interactions with researchers and making methodologies more stakeholder-friendly.

Developing Theories of Change and Logic Models. Articulating a logical set of goals and objectives can be painstaking work for program staff.

However, we have found in our practice that taking the time to help programs verbalize their implied or subtextual goals and objectives is important for the evaluation and for mainstreaming a way of thinking that focuses on problem-solving approaches. Moving several steps beyond stating a coherent set of goals and objectives is the mapping of a full-scale theory of change. Thinking broadly about change also helps program staff disregard the oversimplified mind-set recently imposed on them by the influx of performance measurement approaches.

Logic models, theories of change, and goals and objectives can make program staff and evaluators alike break out in a cold sweat as they envision long days in meeting rooms trying to facilitate agreement among all parties. Many of us know, however, that the long hours, philosophical arguments, and headaches are usually worth it when everyone can clearly see linkages between and among the problem being addressed, interventions, indicators of change, and intermediate and longer-term outcomes. When a theory of change is not developed and stated, programs may suffer from lack of conceptual clarity, and natural changes in programming that evolve over time do not include attendant modifications to indicators, outcomes, and measures. Facilitating a fully expressed theory of change is a task that often falls in the lap of the evaluator. After all, mapping theory is one of our strengths. Or is it?

Because many textbooks offer up research designs that could only work with laboratory mice in strictly controlled environments, theories of change seem easy. Public health experiments may be as straightforward as randomly selecting a population of diseased people into two groups, providing one group with a new drug, and providing the other group with an alternate treatment. We then track disease progression over time, comparing it with baseline data, between groups and within groups, to understand whether the new drug is effective and whether it seems to work better for one group (say, people in the early stages of disease) than another.

In public health, social work, education, and even medicine, we rarely find such clean opportunities for study. More often, we are dealing with abstract and complicated interventions that seek to ameliorate entrenched health and social problems. Treating substance abuse, preventing child abuse, or creating healthy communities all require complex, multilevel strategies that must be untangled and understood if we are to come to any conclusions about their effectiveness.

Evaluators must come to the field equipped to not only think about these issues themselves but do this thought-work in consort with program staff. This is the hard part. But it is also the fun part, and (better yet) it opens the door to dialogue with program staff and participants; we suggest that this open, thoughtful, challenging dialogue can support the mainstreaming of evaluative methods and thinking.

And so, you ask, how on earth do we train graduate students in not only thinking in a complicated way about theories of change but engage in theory-of-change discussion that results in the mainstreaming of evaluative ideas?

Case studies found in textbooks often provide good examples and, indeed, they may be used to launch meaningful discussions (Joint Committee on Standards for Educational Evaluation, 1994; Patton, 1997; Rossi, Freeman, and Lipsey, 1999; Valente, 2002; Worthen, Sanders, and Fitzpatrick, 1997). More lively examples may come from our own practice, including projects we are working on that are in their early stages. We find that our own examples are not more lively because they are necessarily better than the textbook cases but because we, as teachers, know them well.

Another approach is to find ways to bring programs to the class or even take the class to the program. We recently exploited the fact that a colleague from another region of the country had been asked to design an evaluation of a reproductive health program in Africa. She expressed the desire to collaborate with other researchers to improve her evaluation design, and we responded by asking her to join our class via audio-video Internet conferencing, using PolyComm technology. We drop-shipped a laptop with the necessary software and a video camera directly to her office and convened the class in one of our Iowa Communications Network (ICN) classrooms. A couple of weeks prior to the scheduled session, she provided the class with basic reading material that described the program, the country, and the health problem.

The format of the class was that after introductions, our guest described the program and recent developments and information from her client. Students then had the opportunity to ask her a couple of clarifying questions. Next, we began to develop an interactive set of basic research questions to frame her study. Students suggested questions (for example, "How were advisory committee members selected?" "What ethnicities, organizations, and groups do they represent?"), and the entire group discussed their appropriateness to the overall study objectives, their feasibility, and what sort of information they might result in. With a list of five or six viable questions in hand, we discussed the idea of research question hierarchies, where certain key questions implied a set of related subquestions, as in the example noted parenthetically. The next important step was to focus on a single question and brainstorm about indicators, data collection methods, and analytical approaches.

The students walked away from this exercise excited and with an increased sense of self-efficacy in their own problem-solving and facilitating skills around evaluation. Our colleague on the East Coast had a jump-start on her evaluation design. As a follow-up activity, she has volunteered to return to the class (by Internet again) after her data-collection site visit to report on her in-country efforts and challenges.

We suggest that this exercise helped to embed skills in using a problem-solving approach. Although we conducted this exercise with another researcher, we could just as easily have done it with program staff or a single program representative. We are actively looking for an opportunity to work with a program in this way. Once students learn how to work with other people to create logic models, they can begin to think about how they would do it on their own.

Offering Internships and Graduate Assistantships. Many academic departments offer graduate students opportunities to get involved in evaluations of programs within their field of study. In the best of these programs, students are able to get substantive experience that gives them exposure to program stakeholders, involvement in designing the evaluation and selecting measures, a chance to collect data, and analysis and writing opportunities. Clearly, project needs, including level of complexity, and student training, maturity, ability, and interest, play a role in decision making regarding substantive involvement.

We recall the stories of some of the best and most seasoned evaluators who, armed with basic research skills, plunged waist-deep into their first evaluation with little or no formal evaluation training. Evaluators with formal training also say that they only felt truly confident in their roles once they had actual experience in the field. Fortunately, for new evaluators there is such a high demand for their expertise that they may not need to show new clients a history of related experience. Desperate program directors are all too happy to find someone to whom they can entrust their evaluation.

However, if we want to place evaluators in the world who are able to promote mainstreaming through open, participatory approaches to evaluation, they must be mentored by seasoned researchers who understand and whose work embodies the principles that we agree promote mainstreaming. We recommend (1) the use of interns or paid graduate assistants in all phases of evaluations with active mentoring to hone student skills and facilitate epistemological reckoning and (2) postdoctoral fellowships awarded on a competitive basis to provide more intensive, but mentored, experiences with the intention of furthering evaluation methods and fostering thinking about mainstreaming of evaluation. These two recommendations are described next.

A critical element of graduate training is usually time spent working, usually on a research project, with faculty in their area of expertise. Students provide needed support to faculty, and faculty provide students with opportunities for fieldwork, data analysis, and publishing. In the best of situations, students get a substantive research experience, a project they can use for their thesis or dissertation, and a chance to publish.

Evaluation research provides an excellent opportunity for faculty-student collaborations because it is practical and multifaceted and often mixes multiple research methods. It also transfers a real and marketable skill to young professionals who can parlay their graduate work into well-paying external or internal evaluation consultation. Students can be exposed to organizational politics if they attend meetings and learn from their mentors how to handle the delicate situations that frequently arise.

To maximize the assistantship for both faculty and the student, we recommend the following, based on our experiences in academia and the private sector with graduate students and research assistants:

- Set clear expectations for the assistantship, including number of hours per week, meeting attendance (including dress code, if applicable), and products to be developed.
- Establish a schedule for regular meetings to make certain that all staff are on the same page and that the student has enough opportunity to ask questions.
- Hold regular brainstorming sessions to give the student freedom with new ideas and to allow for group problem solving.
- Insist that students do some sort of regular journal-keeping exercise or even Web-logging (blogging) to encourage epistemological thinking.
- State requirements and rules regarding the authorship of publications up-front. Students should get fair credit for their contributions when merited.
- Encourage them to speak or to present posters at conferences. This can be a meaningful way of providing them with autonomy and a chance to gain a new experience.

Finally, we have found it helpful, when possible, to give students a portion of the evaluation that can be entirely their own. We presently have two students who have taken portions of larger evaluations on as part of their preceptorships. One student is starting an in-depth case study of a health clinic to better understand the clinic's process in establishing itself as a medical home for children with special health care needs. Another is focusing on the diffusion of innovation and organizational readiness to change among substance abuse treatment agencies in Iowa that are adopting a new evidence-based practice.

Offering Postgraduate Fellowships and Mentorship Awards. We recommend that the AEA lead an effort to develop a system or network of postgraduate training opportunities to hone the skills of young professionals and academics who want to work in the field of evaluation. The idea would be that postgraduates could receive mentorship and training, either at a university or with an institution (for example, a foundation or a private research consulting company) on a merit basis. Postgraduates at either the master's or doctoral level, depending on the award, would compete for awards that would support their work with a mentor in a particular area of evaluation research. Awards could be made in the areas of social services, public health and medicine, and education. A special award could be made each year to support one postgraduate or doctoral student to work directly with an identified expert in the field of evaluation research, perhaps the president of the AEA.

There may be little difference in the substance of an internship or graduate assistantship and a postgraduate fellowship, except in intensity. The expectations for a postgraduate fellow are clearly higher and would carry the intent that the fellow would be able to conduct his or her own research project from beginning to end with less intervention from the faculty adviser. The final product would be a substantive technical report and an article in a peer-reviewed publication.

A significant addition to the current means of attracting and hiring postgraduate fellows in evaluation would be to offer a significant, merit-based award to attract a top-quality student. The award could be sponsored by a funder (for example, a foundation or government agency) with an interest in nurturing good evaluators or by a private company that might be interested in hiring better-trained evaluators for consulting work.

There are good, existing models for programs like this. For example, the Johnson & Johnson Evaluation Technical Assistance Program pairs Johnson & Johnson Community Health Care Program grantees with graduate students selected from the Johns Hopkins University's Bloomberg School of Public Health doctoral students. The doctoral students are supervised by Hopkins faculty advisers. They provide evaluation technical assistance to grantees in key areas such as refining goals and objectives, identifying useful data sources and data-collection methods, developing survey instruments and databases, analyzing data, and writing reports.

Similarly, the Robert Wood Johnson Foundation Health and Society Scholars Program at the University of Pennsylvania has the goal of creating leaders in the health sciences who are able to produce scholarship, create infrastructure, and design and evaluate interventions at the community level.

Although neither of these programs explicitly aims to promote the mainstreaming of evaluation, both provide ample opportunity to do so. It would also be possible, through similar programs, to not only explicitly state an aim of mainstreaming evaluation but to test that aim through meta-evaluative approaches.

Conclusion

Training for facilitating mainstreaming must be a focused and intensive activity that is participatory and analytical. Those involved in organizational activities and those conducting evaluations need formal training in program evaluation that can be conducted as in-service or preservice training. Those involved in organizational activities need to understand evaluation approaches, know how to interact with evaluators, and have reasonable expectations of what evaluation can and cannot do. Changes in the field of evaluation over the past several years now make mainstreaming evaluation a clear possibility. There is a need to identify the attributes and characteristics of evaluators who can be meaningful participants in mainstreaming evaluation, and these should be used in the admission of trainees into formal evaluation programs.

There is much to do in the design and delivery of evaluation training to prepare organizational personnel and evaluators to work together in a participatory manner, when the evaluation is based on agreed-upon, grounded, and interactive models of program theory and logic. Such training must involve real-world experiences or simulations that reflect reality of settings, dynamics, and interactions. Building in such training experiences requires creativity and capitalization of opportunities for real-world involvement. Not only are such activities the best ways to impart critical competencies and dispositions but they are the ones students enjoy and value the most. Mechanisms need to be established whereby best practices in evaluation training can be identified and shared through the AEA and other organizations.

References

Fetterman, D. M. *Foundations of Empowerment Evaluation.* Thousand Oaks, Calif.: Sage, 2001.

Fetterman, D. M., Shakeh, J., Kaftarian, S., and Wandersman, A. *Empowerment Evaluation: Knowledge and Tools for Self-Assessment and Accountability.* Thousand Oaks, Calif.: Sage, 1996.

Joint Committee on Standards for Educational Evaluation. *The Program Evaluation Standards: How to Assess Evaluations of Educational Programs.* (2nd ed.) Thousand Oaks, Calif.: Sage, 1994.

Lowman, J. *Mastering the Techniques of Teaching.* San Francisco: Jossey-Bass, 1995.

Patton, M. Q. *Utilization-Focused Evaluation.* Thousand Oaks, Calif.: Sage, 1997.

Rossi, P. H., Freeman, H. E., and Lipsey, M. W. *Evaluation: A Systematic Approach.* Thousand Oaks, Calif.: Sage, 1999.

Valente, T. *Evaluating Health Promotion Programs.* New York: Oxford University Press, 2002.

Wallerstein, N. "Power Between Evaluator and Community: Research Relationships Within New Mexico's Healthier Communities." *Social Science and Medicine,* 1999, *49,* 39–43.

Wallerstein, N. "A Participatory Evaluation Model for Healthier Communities: Developing Indicators for New Mexico." *Public Health Reports,* 2000, *115,* 119–204.

Worthen, B. R., Sanders, J. R., and Fitzpatrick, J. L. *Program Evaluation: Alternative Approaches and Practical Guidelines.* Reading, Mass.: Addison-Wesley, 1997.

J. JACKSON BARNETTE is associate professor of community and behavioral health and director of the Center for Public Health Program Evaluation at the University of Iowa College of Public Health. He also serves as associate dean for education and student affairs and director of the master's program in public health in the College of Public Health. He served as chair of the AEA Presidential Strand on Mainstreaming in 2001.

ANNE BABER WALLIS is assistant professor of community and behavioral health and associate director of the Center for Public Health Program Evaluation at the University of Iowa College of Public Health.

6

The authors attended the plenary sessions, several Presidential Strand sessions, and other sessions at the 2001 annual meeting of the AEA to collect examples of evaluators and their clients exploring related issues. The authors raised questions and proposed directions to consider in using evaluation to improve organizations and their practices. Many of their ideas about what mainstreaming means, whether we should mainstream evaluation or not, how evaluation approaches relate to mainstreaming, and how to mainstream are summarized here.

Issues and Practices Related to Mainstreaming Evaluation: Where Do We Flow from Here?

David D. Williams, Mark L. Hawkes

Sanders (2002) noted in his presidential address to the AEA that mainstreaming evaluation depends on institutionalization and capacity building as necessary but not sufficient conditions. He defined mainstreaming evaluation as "the process of evaluation becoming an integral part of the everyday operations of an organization" (p. 254) and raised several questions about it:

Why hasn't evaluation become second nature?
How does mainstreaming of evaluation occur?
What stops mainstreaming of evaluation from occurring?
What difference does mainstreaming make?
Should mainstreaming be universal?
What does mainstreamed evaluation look like?
What are the costs of not mainstreaming evaluation?
What should AEA members do about all this?

Forty-one presentations at the meeting provided examples of evaluators and their clients exploring related issues, raising their own questions, and proposing directions to consider in using evaluation to improve organizations and their practices. Many of these ideas are summarized thematically in four categories: (1) what mainstreaming means, (2) whether we should mainstream evaluation or not, (3) how evaluation approaches relate to mainstreaming, and (4) how to mainstream.

What Mainstreaming Means

Based on the presentations in the Presidential Strand sessions, a consensus regarding what mainstreaming evaluation means is growing around Sanders's article (2002), which is based on his presidential address. In the article, Sanders focuses on mainstreaming evaluation into organizations as a "core value" (p. 257), "an integral part of the everyday operations" (p. 254), and a central "part of the culture and job responsibilities at all levels of the organization" (p. 254) rather than being an add-on or externality to the program being evaluated. He proposes that evaluation is mainstreamed in an organization when participants have "developed a consensus around the use of evaluation to help [them] move toward [their] goals, mission, and vision" (p. 256). Ideally, evaluation is mainstreamed in an organization when it is on every agenda, when evaluation involves roles for those not traditionally affiliated with evaluation activities, when buyers ask for evaluation data on all their purchases, when the CEO distributes a list of organization values that includes continuous evaluation, when orientation for new employees includes their role in evaluating services and products, and when evaluation advocacy is a criterion for orienting new staff.

Grudens-Schuck's presentation (2001) took an anthropological perspective to explore how evaluation cultures develop in organizations and projects. She noted that mainstreaming of evaluation may involve changing organizational cultures, which can be very challenging. Wandersman, Flaspohler, and Ace (2001) defined mainstreaming as helping educational program participants see evaluation as a foundation for making programs work.

Picciotto (2001, 2002) noted that *the mainstream* is the principal course of activity or major current of opinion, and as a noun it means going with the flow, bucolically. But the verb *mainstreaming* suggests dynamic, invasive, almost subversive action, not a soft option. Therefore, we should expect mainstreaming evaluation to be resisted and risky but essential. He also noted the need for both internal and external evaluation components to ensure checks and balances and both vertical and horizontal support for evaluation to truly mainstream it.

Rallis (2001), King (2001a), and Patton (2001a) focused mostly on how to deal with resistance to mainstreaming, helping define it as working with people to make evaluation part of what they do and want to do. Sandoval (2001) described mainstreaming as balance between requirements to evaluate and leadership to inspire and guide participants to actually conduct evaluations and use the results to improve.

Gray (2001) reiterated the importance of evaluation being central to an organization's culture and argued that evaluations must be regular (whether or not they are associated with a particular organization), continuous, collaborative, doable, and viewed as helpful learning opportunities if they are to be considered mainstreamed. One approach to promoting cultural change appears to lie in Gray's ideas of co-evaluation, when a holistic approach to determining organizational effectiveness is taken. Co-evaluation encourages evaluation practices in which funders, administrators, program staff, and evaluators engage collaboratively. What co-evaluation may require of evaluators is an adaptation to the cultural vernacular of the organization in which they work and a gradual introduction of appropriate evaluation language that is useful to clients. Working with participants in the evaluation environment to encourage a process of co-evaluation can create new organizational evaluative roles.

Bielefeldt and Tucker (2001) expanded on last year's theme (2000) of capacity building as one important form of mainstreaming. Andersen and Schwandt (2001) noted that because evaluation is a moral and political matter, evaluation mainstreaming is, too. Therefore, whether and how to mainstream are value-laden choices of agents associated with particular situations.

Scriven (2001a) called for more systematic assembling of results from evaluations, with defensible conclusions that can be depended on as a key part of mainstreaming. He also noted that nonevaluators have learned important evaluation lessons, and their tacit knowledge about the language and culture of an organization, relationships, and networks within an organization provide salient information that should be extracted and shared as well. Scriven also argued that mainstreaming involves being proactive in including evaluation in any work we hear about, supporting clients in finding ways to use reported results, educating people about evaluation from kindergarten through college, and getting involved politically to promote evaluation as an autonomous service discipline. Stake (2001) questioned the practicality of these ideas in mainstreaming, and Stufflebeam (2001a) noted that the ongoing debates he and his colleagues have had constitute the mainstream of evaluation development, which could also be viewed as the mainstream in which evaluation might have an influence.

Several presenters (Nagao, 2001; Ofir, 2001; and Beywl, 2001) noted how mainstreaming is being defined as government requirements for evaluation in Japan, overcoming conflicts between government agencies, development donor organizations, and nongovernment organizations (NGOs) in South Africa, and getting more people trained to be evaluators to meet a growing interest in evaluation in Germany. These panelists included agreement on and use of evaluation standards and the certification of evaluators as promising elements of a mainstreamed evaluation perspective. Patton (2001b) argued that mainstreaming should *not* be confused with mandated evaluation because it will likely yield surface adoption of evaluation and mediocre work. Mandates lead to resistance by many, then a mad cycle of pressuring. Trying to overcome the resulting resistance leads to something other than mainstreaming.

In summary, the many presentations appeared to agree that mainstreaming involves using evaluation results to improve practice and ask better questions, overcome resistance to worthy evaluation efforts, respond to local experience (positive and negative), build an evaluation culture, capacity, and a common language, provide leadership for all of this, build on how people relate to one another, and much more. Using the stream analogy, the Presidential Strand participants viewed mainstreaming as the merging of two or more rivers into one. The evaluation river developed, and as it evolves among social scientists and consultants it should blend wisely with the cultural, organizational, and political rivers of our societies. But there are warnings and cautions, too, some of which are explored briefly in the next section.

Problems with Mainstreaming

The majority of presenters appeared to believe that evaluation should be mainstreamed into organizations and society as a common good. Sanders (2002) typified this near-consensus in the introduction to his presentation, when he asked if evaluation had become second nature yet and then lamented that it had not. However, later he asked if there are settings in which mainstreaming evaluation would not be desirable, and this concern was echoed by a small minority of subsequent speakers.

Grudens-Schuck (2001) claimed evaluation mainstreaming can be a good thing but mainstreaming also raises problems, is much more difficult to achieve than most people think, may require a crisis to get going, and can't really be controlled, though it might be shaped.

Picciotto (2001) argued for mainstreaming but noted several risks and challenges; he concluded that avoiding it would be even riskier. In today's volatile economic and social environment, mainstreaming new concepts is a necessity, but because it breaks valued traditions, disrupts alliances, and weakens the bonds of stakeholder loyalty, it can undermine the stability of the thing being evaluated. Evaluation stakeholders may also have difficulty weighing the opportunity costs of evaluation, believing perhaps, that funds allocated to evaluation might be better suited for program development. If mainstreaming fails, careers may be hurt and reputations damaged. He noted that "being right too early is another way of being wrong" (a French saying), and evaluators are often in this category.

Picciotto (2001) claimed that mainstreaming is hard to achieve because it seeks a new order, is opposed by the mainstream, and calls for innovation. Often symbolic or ceremonial evaluation mainstreaming occurs, such as claiming an evaluation was done but either doing nothing about it or sitting on the results. Readiness to change is critical to the success of mainstreaming. Evaluation facilitates mainstreaming, but it must also be mainstreamed to succeed. Picciotto (2001) identified several obstacles to mainstreaming evaluation, such as opposition by vested interests, lack of leadership, poor incentives, lack of a participatory tradition, path dependence, and obliteration by incorporation (Merton, 1996).

King (2001a) noted that resistance to evaluation is sometimes very appropriate and found an Internet site listing fifty reasons not to do evaluation, which were given by people involved with programs associated with the United Nations. The discovery of these anti-evaluation points reveals a resistance and perhaps some good reasons *not* to hope for mainstreaming of evaluation, even though she joined her fellow presenters to argue for overcoming these sources of resistance.

Building on themes rooted in the dialogue of social justice, Andersen and Schwandt (2001) asked if mainstreaming evaluation, "the practice of establishing evaluation as a central (perhaps even an essential?) technology and ideology in social institutions) is an unqualified social good?" (p. 1). Rather than rush to mainstream so-called value-neutral social science that has been the foundation of evaluation, they argued we should be seeing the mainstreaming issue as a moral-political question. As such, "issues of what it is right to do and good to be in one's dealings with another human being are implicated in the mainstreaming of evaluation practices" (p. 1). Therefore, they urged us to turn "the evaluative gaze onto the very idea of evaluation itself" and to ask if we "*should* mainstream evaluation" (p. 2). They concluded "that, first, we must be clear on just what kind of evaluation practice is being mainstreamed, and we must ask, what are the moral-political consequences of this way of thinking and acting? Second. . . . it is the obligation of those who call themselves evaluators to engage in the kind of deconstructive critique and examination that exposes these consequences" (pp. 7–8). Further, they "advocate[d] for a critical dialogue on the idea of mainstreaming evaluation in society with vigorous participation by different social actors" and "not confined to intellectuals talking among themselves or to ministerial officials" (p. 8). This discussion should "[unfold] in multiple places—for example in discussions within union organizations, user groups, and so on—and through a variety of media (newspapers, televised debates, and interviews, etc.) and [continue] over time" (p. 8). They noted, "From a pedagogical point of view, this is a way of mainstreaming evaluation as well—making the discourse on evaluation an occasion for criticism and possibly transformation of social practices" (p. 8).

Patton (2001b) noted that mainstreaming evaluation can be harmful if it tolerates or encourages only simple monitoring processes. In this case, mainstreaming has the effect of serving accountability purposes at the expense of formative uses for which it is often most useful. However, by using meaningful methods that encourage collaboration and stakeholder participation, evaluation can be productively mainstreamed.

Taken as a whole, these critiques noted the risks and the potential hazards of mainstreaming but actually urged thoughtful pursuit of the concept. However, in some situations, evaluators or those interested in evaluation may have to conclude it cannot be done right now or in the most helpful way.

How Various Evaluation Approaches Relate to Mainstreaming

Many evaluation models are represented by various proponents along the mainstreaming continuum, including everything from utilization-focused (Patton, 1997) to empowerment (Fetterman, 1996), context, input, process, and product (CIPP) evaluation (Stufflebeam, 1971), responsive case study (Stake, 1995), and participatory evaluation (Cousins and Whitmore, 1998) to outcome measurement embedded in a theory-driven evaluation model. This latter extreme was described by Fischer (2001), who illustrated how evaluation strategies and foci can transfer to other program areas within and between agencies to make evaluation a more systemic part of family development programming.

Sanders (2002) noted that although some approaches, such as accreditation, indicate a commitment to evaluation by organizations, these approaches do not guarantee sustainable use of evaluation that would be typical of mainstreamed evaluation. He referred to capacity building and noted a growing array of practices to improve the quality and use of evaluation but concluded that we can build capacity to evaluate without making evaluation part of our culture, which mainstreamed evaluation would be. He also asked if mainstreaming is the same as participatory evaluation, raising the question of whether evaluation approaches that involve people affected by evaluations and by the programs being evaluated in conducting parts or all of those evaluations will also lead to or constitute the cultural change he associates with mainstreaming evaluation.

Andersen and Schwandt (2001) and Owen (2001) noted that approaches to evaluation involve much more than how data are collected. Different approaches also include values, though usually not explicitly, and positions on who evaluation is for, how evaluation should affect relationships, and other assumptions about the culture in which evaluation is being promoted. Owen noted that we cannot talk about evaluation as a single entity any more. We need to acknowledge many different meanings and decide which we value the most before mainstreaming can be done thoughtfully.

Mabry (2001) invited proponents of different approaches to explore theories of action that underpin these approaches. Stufflebeam (2001b), Patton (2001c), Fetterman (2001a), Greene (2001), and Scriven (2001b) explored this question and seemed to conclude that although they have taken very different approaches in the evaluations they conduct, they all believe their ideas are built on the assumption that participants should be able to use the results of evaluations based on their approaches to work better and produce better results. In this sense, the various approaches are built on theories of action, which would imply that they are compatible with mainstream evaluation purposes, as outlined by Sanders (2002).

But if the various approaches are compatible with mainstreaming, why is evaluation not mainstreamed already? Scriven argued (2001a) that it is because evaluators are not taking their knowledge-keeping responsibilities seriously; they are not proactive enough in getting evaluation included as part of new initiatives or in giving support beyond the reporting phase to their clients who want to implement results; they do not provide people with enough education about the value of evaluation, and they are not politically active or sensitive enough to get information out to people who can use it. Scriven's criticisms apply to all the approaches to evaluation assembled by Mabry.

Sandoval (2001) and Wandersman, Flaspohler, and Ace (2001) argued that although accreditation pressure is not the ideal form of evaluation, we can and should use that very real political tool to mainstream evaluation. In conjunction with other approaches, including strong leadership, accreditation requirements can encourage reluctant participants to include evaluation in their daily work until other internal motivations to reflect on performance grow to maturity and evaluation becomes more central to their cultures.

Picciotto (2001) briefly reviewed six different approaches to evaluation and then argued that, rather than fight among ourselves about the best way to conduct or conceptualize evaluations, we must cooperate and have more mainstreaming of views about what evaluation is and how to do it within the evaluation community before we can really hope to mainstream evaluation into the broader culture. The potential for mainstreaming evaluation may lie in how those in the evaluation discipline agree on their own methodologies, epistemologies, and roles within the organizations they work.

Sanders (2002) asked if participatory evaluation *is* mainstreamed evaluation because it involves the participants in evaluation as part of the many other dimensions of their program activities. Grudens-Schuck (2001) described her short cultural study of a ten-year participatory evaluation in Indonesia. She reported that the participants were not only *not* conducting the participatory study but that the evaluation conducted was external and nonparticipatory. In one sense, this finding suggested that an evaluation culture of some sort had been established but not around a particular approach to evaluation. Perhaps versions of participatory evaluation are compatible with mainstreaming, but by no means does that approach guarantee mainstreaming an evaluation culture.

Gray (2001) presented an approach she called "co-evaluation" that is continuous and collaborative and involves organizational culture and participant learning, as well as integration of external evaluators as co-investigators with internal participants. This and other participatory approaches appear to be engaged in mainstreaming by involving participants in doing the evaluation as well as receiving it from others. We need to know more about how well those approaches are working, how they are defining mainstreaming, and what the benefits are.

Several presenters (Lamdany, 2001; Imas, 2001; Rist, 2001; Grasso, 2001; Nagao, 2001; Ofir, 2001; and Patton, 2001d) emphasized the need to continue engaging people from different countries and cultures in discussions about what counts as evaluation and what would constitute mainstreaming of evaluation in those situations. Clearly, evaluation approaches that are incompatible with a culture will never be mainstreamed into that culture.

Stufflebeam (2001a), Scriven (2001a), Stake (2001), and Sanders (2001a) highlighted the fact that evaluation theorists have been advocating mainstreaming of evaluation for years by building meta-evaluation into the evaluation process, engaging the stakeholders in voicing their values, and so on. The Joint Committee on Standards for Educational Evaluation (1994) and the American Evaluation Association's Principles (Shadish, Newman, Scheirer, and Wye, 1995) both encourage ongoing examination of how well evaluation is meeting the integral needs of evaluation recipients. They argue that this self-examination fulfills critical elements of mainstreaming.

Stufflebeam (2001a) also reviewed an evaluation conducted over three decades ago to illustrate the important role evaluators must take in achieving mainstreaming of evaluation. When working at the Ohio State University, he was approached by the Columbus public schools in 1965 to provide evaluation assistance that was mandated with the receipt of $6 million from the federal government. With no expertise of their own for such evaluation activities, the district superintendent correctly assumed that the university would be more than willing to accommodate them if 10 percent of the budget were allocated to the effort. However, as Stufflebeam related, the superintendent erred in thinking that the evaluation would be of little practical value or that the evaluators would be content to keep out of the district's way as the university administered tests and implemented a quasi-experimental evaluation. Stufflebeam's new evaluation center agreed to the evaluation contract only if the superintendent would support an evaluation mainstreaming effort to prepare about a dozen Columbus teachers to staff a new district evaluation office. The superintendent reluctantly agreed, and by the end of the three-year project, a district-level office had been formed and was staffed by district personnel with advanced degrees and significant practical experience. These evaluators remained with the district, produced nationally recognized evaluations, and served as officers of national educational and evaluation organizations. The Columbus public schools illustration is not only one of concentrated capacity building toward mainstreaming evaluation but it suggests that mainstreaming may require intense, determined negotiation.

In summary, no approach to evaluation has been singled out as being incompatible with mainstreaming. Rather, an openness to alternative approaches, with sensitivity to the needs of organizations and participants and an awareness of how different kinds of evaluation might enhance daily work, seems most desirable. Combinations of approaches as diverse as accreditation (externally driven) to self-evaluation of various forms may lead to mainstreaming in alternative settings. Issues such as leadership, knowledge sharing, political activism, and assumptions about values may be more critical to mainstreaming than particular evaluation approaches.

How to Mainstream Evaluation

Key issues in developing mainstreamed evaluation include responding to local experience with evaluation (positive and negative), understanding the organizational culture with an eye to building an evaluation culture, building capacity to conduct and use evaluation, providing leadership, acquiring a sophisticated understanding of how people relate to one another, and other contextual details. Ideas for addressing these issues are discussed next in terms of involving evaluation consumers, understanding the need for building and using better evaluation theory, balancing compulsion and volunteerism to evaluate, and becoming more aware of culture and how to change it.

Work with Consumers. Underlying all other suggestions for mainstreaming are the identification of people who could use evaluation to enhance their work and working with them in appropriate ways to build evaluation into what they do.

Duignan (2001) claimed evaluation has been marginalized in many cultures. In his paper, he explored reasons why evaluation has been marginalized and what mainstreaming might look like if marginalization could be overcome. He argued that evaluation is often either oversimplified or made overly complex and that if evaluation itself is to become mainstreamed, it must first mainstream (that is, put into terms the participants commonly use) the conclusions and subsequent recommendations it suggests to organizations. He felt that marginalization is at least partially a product of the professionalization of evaluators, which sets them apart from rather than incorporates them into society. He shared a counterexample from the health sector in New Zealand, where evaluators have learned to work as equals with their program clients and professionals. He concluded that evaluations should be responsive to the contexts in which they are done.

Picciotto (2001) reviewed three types of social actors who must work together to achieve mainstreaming and claimed that for evaluations to have the most influence, all three of these actors are required:

- *Connectors,* who have easy access to large numbers of influential acquaintances
- *Mavens,* who specialize in accumulating and disseminating accurate and timely knowledge
- *Salesmen,* who have the intuition, knowledge, and energy to persuade and motivate

Obviously, connectors and salesmen are focused on working with consumers, whereas much of evaluation has been focused on the maven task. Mainstreaming will only come through working with people more effectively. Another implication is that evaluators should capitalize on existing or easily obtained access points, or people who already play the connector and salesman roles in society, organizations, and the cultures they serve. One example offered by Ofir (2001) was the suggestion to use relationships with donors to encourage them to make evaluation part of their funding requirements.

Scriven (2001a) urged better reporting strategies to make evaluation reports more accessible, transparent, and useful to those who will read them so they can more readily integrate the results into their practices. He identified possible ways to share what is being learned through databases, technologies, and collaborative relationships.

Scriven (2001a) also urged evaluators to reach out to their audiences from kindergarten on to systematically educate the public about evaluation issues. He suggested using courses, public media, and other educational resources to help people know who evaluators are and why society needs them. His premise was that the field of evaluation should realize that and act as if mainstreaming were an essential part of evaluation. To do this, Scriven notes, involves educating and re-educating leaders and other key cultural contacts who can influence the use of evaluation in all aspects of society.

A few writers (for example, Nagao, 2001; Beywl, 2001) assumed or encouraged the use of evaluator certification as something many consumers recognize. At least some feel evaluators should continue to talk about and consider evaluator certification as one way people in the mainstream might recognize and accept evaluation as part of their culture.

Gray (2001) and Sanders (2001b) both suggested that a key element of mainstreaming is building a common language. Gray argued that this building involves evaluators working to understand the perspectives of evaluation consumers and combining that understanding with their own views to establish a language common to both evaluators and those they serve. She maintained that since most organizations have proven willing to adopt, at least in part, evaluation terminology (for example, *formative, summative, meta-evaluation*), evaluators must be willing to adopt the language of their clients as well.

Sanders (2001b) included language as an element in a common culture and the sharing of common values:

> I continue to look at mainstreaming as adopting evaluation as a core value of an organization or a professional practice. Evaluation must become part of the culture, building a common language. If these things happen, evaluation behavior will follow. Changes in values lead to changes in behavior. The question about what we are asking people to mainstream is a critical question. To

> me we are asking people to mainstream a frame of mind, to ask good questions, be skeptical, use answers to bring about change, to continue to move toward excellence in practice.

In summary, there are multiple ways to engage with evaluation consumers—by building a common vocabulary, becoming more people-oriented, using educational opportunities and reporting requirements to communicate better with more potential participants, and many more. The thrust of this theme, though, is that evaluators need to pay more attention to consumers of their evaluations if there is to be any hope of mainstreaming.

Build and Use Theory. Many of the ideas shared elsewhere in this summary allude to the importance of building and using theory that takes mainstreaming issues into account. Some presenters illustrated an action theory of change in their own work. For instance, the description Silver (2001) gave of mainstreamed evaluation in a highly visible not-for-profit service agency included the assistance of evaluators in helping partner entities integrate performance objectives and success indicators as a part of their service goals. This mainstreamed evaluation activity resulted in the evolution of program logic models that help focus and coordinate multiagency service.

Similarly, Harris (2001), who conducts evaluation activities in the juvenile justice system of a large urban area, described a process of mainstreaming outcome data into a tracking program for delinquent youths that has resulted in significant strides in making decisions and developing policy around correctional, judicial, prosecutorial, and rehabilitation issues. From his experience at the World Bank, Picciotto (2001) suggested that a theory of mainstreaming may be "embedded" in a web of information networks and social links that exist in an organization. Framed in a theory of human interaction, evaluation may at the same time be hierarchical, individualistic, and relational.

A few authors addressed the point about theory more overtly, suggesting evaluation theorists and all practitioners ought to examine their own theoretical foundations in light of mainstreaming concerns. For example, Sanders (2002), Picciotto (2001), Sandoval (2001), Gray (2001), Hunter and Kaye (2001), Andersen and Schwandt (2001), and Greene (2001) identified the phenomenon of change as central to the concept of mainstreaming. Patton (2001b, 2001c) noted that change theory as formed in many fields (for example, organizational change, learning, change adoption, economic theory, findings use, contingency theory, marketing theory, social theory) may help guide some cultures to include evaluation as integral. Evaluators should take the literature on change theory seriously, use their experiences to build grounded theory, and put that theory into practice (Grudens-Schuck, 2001).

Scriven (2001a) and Ofir (2001) urged evaluators to learn from current evaluation experiences as well as literature on theory. People within the evaluation world (formal evaluators but also many who conduct informal evaluations or are clients for evaluations) have learned important lessons. It is important to capture those lessons and integrate them into lessons for mainstreaming evaluation.

Others (for example, Owen, 2001; Fetterman, 2001a) noted that in addition to learning from experienced evaluators and clients, evaluators should continue to expand definitions of evaluation to be more inclusive of multiple perspectives. Three authors (Nagao, 2001; Ofir, 2001; Beywl, 2001), reviewing approaches and challenges to evaluation in Japan, South Africa, and Germany, respectively, highlighted the importance of continuing an international dialogue and including what is learned in evaluation theory development. Likewise, including mainstreaming as an integral and perpetual part of evaluation will involve educating and re-educating evaluators, organizational leaders, and others who can influence the use of evaluation in their settings.

Several authors (Sanders, 2002; Gray, 2001; Hunter and Kaye, 2001; Nagao, 2001; Ofir, 2001; Conner, 2001) noted the problems with and the need to balance internal and external evaluation roles and to examine their impact on mainstreaming. They argued that evaluators need to explore how these two roles interact even more and build what they learn into evaluation theory and practice. Picciotto (2001) elaborated on this topic by discussing the process of intra-organizational or "horizontal" mainstreaming. This within-program evaluation may require organizational (internal) independence; however, that independence should not be construed either as isolation or as a possible compromise to external evaluation. In fact, Picciotto (2001) argued that important internal organizational safeguards are at work when a combination of internal and external evaluation is achieved.

Significant capacity is also built into collaborations that combine internal and external evaluation, as described by Hunter and Kaye (2001) of the McConnell Foundation. Building the internal capacity for evaluation of grantees in youth services and coupling that capacity with the insight and experience of external evaluators, resulted in stronger programs operating within a more sustainable organization. Balancing the roles of internal and external evaluation seemed to be a critical element in achieving mainstreaming.

Finally, two panels at the 2001 AEA annual meeting (Mabry, 2001; Stufflebeam, 2001a, 2001b; Patton, 2001c; Fetterman, 2001a; Greene, 2001; Scriven, 2001a, 2001b; Stake, 2001; Sanders, 2001a) reminded evaluators that theorists have been addressing mainstreaming issues for many years and they deserve more attention. For example, both the AEA's Guiding Principles and the Joint Committee's Standards reflect the theories of many evaluators and call for specific actions that would enhance mainstreaming if they were followed. For instance, the first Standard focuses on identifying and responding to the particular needs of stakeholders. The five Guiding Principles (see "Responsibilities for

General and Public Welfare") do the same, indicating that evaluation could become more mainstreamed into the cultures of those stakeholders if stakeholders' views were honored. Likewise, the existence of the Principles and the Standards reflects a strong theoretical basis for urging evaluators and the consumers of evaluation to conduct meta-evaluations; such studies would encourage improved evaluation processes.

Along these same lines, to the extent that mainstreaming becomes a theoretical component of evaluation, perhaps we need evaluation of mainstreaming built into all meta-evaluations. How well are our evaluations encouraging attitudes and cultural perspectives that will support evaluative thinking? In a related vein, participatory approaches appear to be engaged in mainstreaming by involving participants in doing the evaluation as well as receiving it from others.

Involvement of stakeholders was the approach taken by Bielefeldt and Tucker (2001) in a U.S. Department of Education, Office of Postsecondary Education grant. The evaluators sought to develop the capacity of school teachers to apply the protocols and processes of evaluation into their own technology integration work. This effort to make teachers aware of the critical elements of technology integration resulted in teachers becoming more aware of and more inclined to incorporate evaluation into their practice. Moreover, these teachers then focused on all parts of the technology integration program and not just on students' outcomes. We need to know more about how well those approaches are working, how they are defining mainstreaming, and what the benefits and costs are.

In summary, theories of evaluation have dealt indirectly with mainstreaming for many years. These sessions suggest that the evaluation community should examine current theory and take associated injunctions to heart. In addition, more effort should be made to explore current practice and alternatives as theories are developed and practices follow suit.

Maintain Balance Between Compulsion and Volunteerism. As Patton (2001b) noted, there is a tension between mandates for evaluation and leadership that encourages people to voluntarily seek evaluative guidance for their choices:

> I heard several presentations with the interest focused on accountability and mandating of evaluation. People are responding to mandates in many settings, often under the cover of mainstreaming. We have evidence that such mandates typically lead to surface adoption and mediocre work. Social change theory suggests force doesn't work. It is more in the nature of things to create resistance when we seek to force. I urge people not to mandate or confuse mandating with mainstreaming. I'm convinced less is more and we need quality rather than quantity in mainstreaming; and mandating does just the opposite.

Engle (2001), Rallis (2001), King (2001a), and Patton (2001a) addressed resistance directly in a 2001 AEA panel session, acknowledging that people have very good reasons for resisting evaluation. These authors and others (for example, Ofir, 2001) suggest that dealing with resistance in helpful ways is essential for moving evaluation into the mainstream. This strategy involves such practices as understanding why there is resistance, building trust over time, and capitalizing on pressures without becoming part of the pressure.

The consensus among several presenters (Picciotto, 2001; Patton, 2001a and 2001d; Sandoval, 2001; Fetterman, 2001b) was that keeping evaluation going beyond mandated versions relies on local capacity being built or on obtaining results people value so that they want more. Evaluators need to employ both bottom-up and top-down efforts to achieve mainstreaming—pressure through requirements from funding agencies but also responsiveness to participants' desires to have voice and improve their situation.

This dual focus on compulsion and the voluntary use of evaluation may require evaluators who are seeking ways to unite them. Compulsion to evaluate (accreditation, legislated accountability, and grant requirements) has been key to continuing evaluation efforts reported by many presenters as successes. But most people agree evaluators must capitalize on continuing requirements the society makes for accountability without letting accountability completely define the evaluation field. Evaluators must resist complete mainstreaming in the sense of "required" evaluation.

Leadership is a critical issue in the balancing act. Picciotto (2001) noted that one major obstacle to mainstreaming evaluation is lack of leadership. Both he and Sandoval (2001) gave case histories illustrating the essential role of leaders who have the vision of how evaluation can benefit their organizations and those they serve. Gray (2001) noted that leaders can remove the onus from evaluation and review as they become evaluative thinkers and embrace evaluation as part of what they do and not as an add-on. Leaders can reward those who accept evaluation and are willing to change in light of evaluation findings while building a climate of trust. But obtaining such leadership involves educating and re-educating formal leaders and others who can influence the use of evaluation.

In summary, leadership is a key to mainstreaming. Even though donors and governments may mandate evaluation, until organizational leaders gain the vision of what evaluation can do and build support among the rank and file, internal evaluation that translates the results of external evaluation into action will not happen and mainstreaming will not occur. Evaluators must work with leaders from where they are.

Be Aware of Culture and Change. A final theme, which has been mentioned in many of the other sections as a subtheme, is the belief of many authors that mainstreaming is a cultural issue. Organizations either have a culture that encourages and is built on evaluation or they don't. So if evaluation is to be mainstreamed into some settings, cultural change must occur. And obtaining such change is not easy. Evaluators must get ready for a challenge or be willing to withdraw if resistance means sacrificing their ethical convictions (Grudens-Schuck, 2001; Picciotto, 2001; Rallis, 2001; Patton, 2001d).

Where Do We Flow from Here?

During the final session of the 2001 AEA conference, Patton (2001b), King (2001b), Conner (2001), and Sanders (2001b) discussed implications and thoughts about the future after hearing a brief summary (the essence of this article) of the Presidential Strand sessions by Williams (2001) and Hawkes (2001). Their thoughts are presented next, briefly, to suggest the future mainstreaming might take.

Patton (2001b) began by noting that it will be interesting to see what the language of mainstreaming brings with it long term. "Maybe we will be able to set an agenda for the field." He was impressed with the extent to which presenters took the theme seriously and believes Sanders has made a major contribution toward setting an agenda with his 2001 AEA presidential address (Sanders, 2002) and sponsoring the Presidential Strand presentations. He felt the common themes among the presentations were that people are struggling to decide whether mainstreaming evaluation is desirable and, if it is, what it will take to get below the surface to the affecting of culture—a dominant challenge.

Patton heard several presentations expressing interest in accountability and the mandating of evaluation, but he doesn't feel mandating will work in the long run. He noted that people are responding to mandates in many settings, often under the cover of mainstreaming, but the evidence appears to show us that such mandates typically lead to surface adoption and mediocre work.

He clarified that the research on diffusion of innovations has greatly influenced his work on utilization-focused evaluation. From this he has concluded that instead of saying everyone has to do it, we should tell people evaluation is hard and possibly really profitable but we want to involve only those who are willing to try and then we'll add more and more resources. "Tell them everyone can't do it! Only those who really want to demonstrate excellence should get involved. Use reverse psychology!"

Patton finished with another water metaphor: John Wesley Powell's first traversing of the Colorado River through the Grand Canyon. He put together an expedition and found some of the most magnificent geography in the world, as well as some of the greatest danger. Powell survived and had a lot of influence on encouraging a research approach to deciding how to use these water resources. "This conference tells us where to enter the canyon and Jim's [Sanders, 2002] talk tells us where we want to come out; but over the next ten to fifteen years we ought to learn what is between and hope we can get through the rapids."

King (2001b) was a bit more pessimistic. She began by telling of a colleague who commented on how King is always smiling.

> I came to AEA excited because mainstreaming is my life's work. I have to say though that I now fear I am drowning! I wonder if mainstreaming is such a great idea, why isn't it happening? I teach introductory evaluation a few thousand times a year and am struck with the fact that we don't know what mainstreaming is but we are still vague about what evaluation is too! So how can we mainstream what we haven't defined? Is that a copout? We don't have many community folk here to tell us what all this might mean in their lives. What's in it for them? There aren't a lot of compulsive evaluators in my world. I had some program staff here for a couple of days and they wondered why people weren't asking them what they thought. People have an intuitive notion of evaluation but what does it take to institutionalize that? If it is to be done, it should be done well and we have many examples of poorly done evaluation. It makes great sense to cheat when there is lots of pressure for schools to have report cards based on tests the students have no motivation to do well on. Resources—where do we find those to do evaluation? Do they follow particular people who believe in evaluation? Especially how do you mainstream in times of scarce resources? Is it possible people will have to give up serving some clients to find resources for evaluation? I will keep smiling but I fear that we don't know how to proceed. We need to get out and talk with our clients to create ongoing evaluation that will live in the organizations we serve.

Conner (2001) used some water metaphors to note that he is working with many different cultures now, rarely with Caucasians.

> I'm working with a Chinese coalition but they are using English to overcome many problems. I'm attending Korean meetings too but they're more traditional and have the Elders attend and they segregate the men. That is a stream I'm stepping into. As our worlds get closer and closer we'll do more and more of this. We have more and more foundation and philanthropic organizations represented here. They have their own streams too. There are lessons and cautions as we become part of the mainstreams.

Some cautions he raised were these:

- Does this imply we're joining the establishment and structure?
- Can we set up guidelines and checks so we don't lose the value of being outside the mainstream?
- We need to learn some new things about our structure and infrastructure.
- There are various contexts, and mainstreaming carries some with it.
- Systems theory has a lot to say about recommending changes, and we ought to know more about that. Be cautious as we get into that and invite the systems theory people to come talk to us.

- The business sector does a lot of evaluation work, but we don't see many of them here and we could benefit more from them and we ought to invite them.

During a discussion with the audience, Patton claimed that the fact that not everyone agrees on what evaluation is isn't a problem.

> The strength of our field is its diversity. Even if we agreed on the term evaluation there are lots of ways to do that. We've demonstrated that we won't agree. Every three months on EvalTalk there will be a new person asking if evaluation is different from research and we will disagree in the ensuing discussion. We do it here too. I don't agree that we can only mainstream if we have a common definition. Evaluative thinking, ways of being explicit and bringing evidence to bear, runs through all kinds of evaluation. The challenge is in the application to different situations. Developing competencies of helping clients fit the type of evaluation to their need is the challenge. We have to get better at understanding core evaluation competencies which include this identification of different approaches.

King agreed and then added that what worries her is that the role of evaluator is on a continuum from stand-alone evaluators to partners to empowered individuals. But most practicing evaluators only use a limited amount of what they know and could use.

Sanders (2001b) concluded the session and 2001 AEA conference by saying,

> I'm pleased with what we've learned from our presenters and panelists. I continue to look at mainstreaming as adopting evaluation as a core value of an organization or a professional practice. Evaluation is becoming part of the culture, a common language. If these things happen, evaluation behavior will follow. Changes in values lead to changes in behavior. The question about what we are asking people to mainstream is a critical question. To me we are asking people to mainstream a frame of mind, to ask good questions, be skeptical, use answers to bring about change, to continue to move toward excellence in practice. What kinds of questions are good questions? We ought to look at goal attainment but also do the right thing and judge the goals and look for better ways to accomplish our ideals and visions. There are higher order values we need to take into account when we question our practices. As evaluators we ought to always be evaluating our evaluations and if they are harmful to practices, we need to terminate or rethink them. That is part of mainstreaming—asking good questions about our own practices. We need to continuously look at alternative points of view. We ought to be benevolently skeptical about our own practices. That is also what we ought to see in an organization that has mainstreamed evaluation.

Conclusion

Streams flow and change. About 500 B.C., Heraclitus pointed out that "upon those who step into the same rivers, different and ever different waters flow down" (*Encyclopedia Britannica*, 5, p. 860). Or, as we say it now, "we can never step into the same stream twice." What about "mainstreams?" Is there "a mainstream" that evaluation might get into? And if it did, would it be the same mainstream tomorrow? Or does mainstreaming imply flexibility—adaptability to an ever-shifting stream?

What about evaluation? There seem to be many kinds of evaluation. Which should or can be mainstreamed into which streams of society? Some views of evaluation suggest we reach into the stream from a bank of objectivity to take out components for analysis and judgment. Others advocate diving in and riding the current with commentaries and advice to and from partners in rafts sailing nearby. And others suggest evaluators must become part of the stream itself, or at least become boulders and banks to have any impact on the flow of the stream.

Most all forms of evaluation mainstreaming seem somewhat analogous to reaching beyond the bank, through the shallows, and into the main flow of the stream while analyzing and judging some aspects of the stream and perhaps even changing the flow or direction of parts of the stream. It might be productive to think these images through as we contemplate our current issues and practices in evaluation mainstreaming and where we ought to flow from here in terms of this metaphor.

We could be carried along by volatile waters, as the topic of mainstreaming evaluations continues to be discussed. But many have suggested that we wade in even further at whatever access points are available to us and not worry about holding the stream still until we can finally define the "right" way to evaluate or to mainstream. We may never encounter exactly the same stream twice, but we cannot wait for flood or drought to make our efforts worthless either!

References

Andersen, L. A., and Schwandt, T. A. "Mainstreaming Evaluation in Society: Understanding the Moral/Political Orientation of Evaluation Practice." Paper presented during session 543 at the annual meeting of the American Evaluation Association, St. Louis, Nov. 9, 2001.

Beywl, W. "New Developments of Evaluation as Profession in the German Speaking Countries." Paper presented during session 701 at the annual meeting of the American Evaluation Association, St. Louis, Nov. 10, 2001.

Bielefeldt, T., and Tucker, S. A. "Evaluating 'Technology Integration' Projects: Learning from Twelve Projects Across the US." Paper presented during session 542 at the annual meeting of the American Evaluation Association, St. Louis, Nov. 9, 2001.

Conner, R. F. "Reflections on Mainstreaming Evaluation." Comments presented during session 790 at the annual meeting of the American Evaluation Association, St. Louis, Nov. 10, 2001.

Cousins, J. B., and Whitmore, E. "Framing Participatory Evaluation." In E. Whitmore (ed.), *Participatory Evaluation Approaches.* San Francisco: Jossey-Bass, 1998.

Duignan, P. "Mainstreaming Evaluation or Building Evaluation Capability? Three Key Elements." Paper presented during session 101 at the annual meeting of the American Evaluation Association, St. Louis, Nov. 7, 2001.

Engle, M. "What's Happening Here? Resistance: Barriers to Mainstreaming, the Psychology in Evaluation." Part of a discussion presented during session 323 at the annual meeting of the American Evaluation Association, St. Louis, Nov. 8, 2001.

Fetterman, D. M. *Empowerment Evaluation: Knowledge and Tools for Self-Assessment and Accountability.* Thousand Oaks, Calif.: Sage, 1996.

Fetterman, D. "Theories of Action in Program Evaluation." Paper presented during session 569 at the annual meeting of the American Evaluation Association, St. Louis, Nov. 9, 2001a.

Fetterman, D. "Why Empowerment Evaluation Is or Needs to Be More Than Mere Internal Evaluation." Part of a debate presented during session 347 at the annual meeting of the American Evaluation Association, St. Louis, Nov. 8, 2001b.

Fischer, R. L. "Making Outcome Data Essential to Nonprofits: Outcomes Measurement and Program Improvement in a Direct-Service Agency." Paper presented during session 346 at the annual meeting of the American Evaluation Association, St. Louis, Nov. 8, 2001.

Grasso, P. G. "Mainstreaming Evaluation on the Development Gateway." Paper presented during session 517 at the annual meeting of the American Evaluation Association, St. Louis, Nov. 9, 2001.

Gray, S. T. "A Key Process for Effective Leaders: Ongoing Evaluation." Paper presented during session 500 at the annual meeting of the American Evaluation Association, St. Louis, Nov. 9, 2001.

Greene, J. C. "Theories of Action in Program Evaluation." Paper presented during session 569 at the annual meeting of the American Evaluation Association, St. Louis, Nov. 9, 2001.

Grudens-Schuck, N. "The Rigidity and Comfort of Habits: A Philosophical and Cultural Analysis of the Ups and Downs of Mainstreaming Evaluation." Paper presented during session 101 at the annual meeting of the American Evaluation Association, St. Louis, Nov. 7, 2001.

Harris, P. "Experiences with Mainstreaming: An Outcome-Based Information System Tracking Delinquent Youths in the City of Philadelphia's Juvenile Justice System." Paper presented during session 346 at the annual meeting of the American Evaluation Association, St. Louis, Nov. 8, 2001.

Hawkes, M. L. "Reflections on Mainstreaming Evaluation." Summary of papers presented during session 790 at the annual meeting of the American Evaluation Association, St. Louis, Nov. 10, 2001.

Hunter, D.E.K., and Kaye, J. "Evaluation as an Inherent Element of Institution Building: A Case Study of Mainstreaming Evaluation." Paper presented during session 501 at the annual meeting of the American Evaluation Association, St. Louis, Nov. 9, 2001.

Imas, L. M. "International Program for Development Evaluation Training." Paper presented during session 517 at the annual meeting of the American Evaluation Association, St. Louis, Nov. 9, 2001.

Joint Committee on Standards for Educational Evaluation. *The Program Evaluation Standards: How to Assess Evaluations of Educational Programs.* (2nd ed.) Thousand Oaks, Calif.: Sage, 1994.

King, J. A. "What's Happening Here? Resistance: Barriers to Mainstreaming, the Psychology in Evaluation." Part of a discussion presented during session 323 at the annual meeting of the American Evaluation Association, St. Louis, Nov. 8, 2001a.

King, J. A. "Reflections on Mainstreaming Evaluation." Comments presented during session 790 at the annual meeting of the American Evaluation Association, St. Louis, Nov. 10, 2001b.

Lamdany, R. "Evaluating Country Assistance Programs." Paper presented during session 517 at the annual meeting of the American Evaluation Association, St. Louis, Nov. 9, 2001.

Mabry, L. "Theories of Action in Program Evaluation." A discussion monitored during session 569 at the annual meeting of the American Evaluation Association, St. Louis, Nov. 9, 2001.

Merton, R. K. *On Social Structure and Science.* (P. Sztompka, ed.). Chicago: University of Chicago Press, 1996.

Nagao, M. "A Japanese Perspective on Evaluation." Paper presented during session 701 at the annual meeting of the American Evaluation Association, St. Louis, Nov. 10, 2001.

Ofir, Z. "A Southern African Perspective on Evaluation." Paper presented during session 701 at the annual meeting of the American Evaluation Association, St. Louis, Nov. 10, 2001.

Owen, J. "Discussant Responding to Andersen and Schwandt." Reactions to a paper presented during session 543 at the annual meeting of the American Evaluation Association, St. Louis, Nov. 9, 2001.

Patton, M. Q. *Utilization-Focused Evaluation.* (3rd ed.) Thousand Oaks, Calif.: Sage, 1997.

Patton, M. Q. "What's Happening Here? Resistance: Barriers to Mainstreaming, the Psychology in Evaluation." Part of a discussion presented during session 323 at the annual meeting of the American Evaluation Association, St. Louis, Nov. 8, 2001a.

Patton, M. Q. "Reflections on Mainstreaming Evaluation." Comments presented during session 790 at the annual meeting of the American Evaluation Association, St. Louis, Nov. 10, 2001b.

Patton, M. Q. "Theories of Action in Program Evaluation." A paper presented during session 569 at the annual meeting of the American Evaluation Association, St. Louis, Nov. 9, 2001c.

Patton, M. Q. "From Emergence to Mainstreaming: Issues and Lessons Learned." A paper presented during session 701 at the annual meeting of the American Evaluation Association, St. Louis, Nov. 10, 2001d.

Picciotto, R. "Evaluation and Mainstreaming: Lessons of Development Experience." Paper presented during session 300 at the annual meeting of the American Evaluation Association, St. Louis, Nov. 8, 2001.

Picciotto, R. "The Logic of Mainstreaming: A Development Evaluation Perspective." *Evaluation,* 2002, *8*(3), 322–339.

Rallis, S. "What's Happening Here? Resistance: Barriers to Mainstreaming, the Psychology in Evaluation." Part of a discussion presented during session 323 at the annual meeting of the American Evaluation Association, St. Louis, Nov. 8, 2001.

Rist, R. "International Development Evaluation Association." Paper presented during session 517 at the annual meeting of the American Evaluation Association, St. Louis, Nov. 9, 2001.

Sanders, J. R. Discussant for session 700 titled "Three Seniors Examine Issues in Mainstreaming Evaluation." Annual meeting of the American Evaluation Association, St. Louis, Nov. 10, 2001a.

Sanders, J. R. "Reflections on Mainstreaming Evaluation." Comments presented during session 790 at the annual meeting of the American Evaluation Association, St. Louis, Nov. 10, 2001b.

Sanders, J. R. "Presidential Address: On Mainstreaming Evaluation." *American Journal of Evaluation,* 2002, *23*(2), 253–259.

Sandoval, P. A. "Meeting New Standards for Teacher Education: Mainstreaming Evaluation in Education." Paper presented during session 390 at the annual meeting of the American Evaluation Association, St. Louis, Nov. 8, 2001.

Scriven, M. "Upgrading the Evaluation Conceptions and Practices of Philanthropy, Academe, and Government." Paper presented during session 700 at the annual meeting of the American Evaluation Association, St. Louis, Nov. 10, 2001a.

Scriven, M. "Theories of Action in Program Evaluation." Paper presented during session 569 at the annual meeting of the American Evaluation Association, St. Louis, Nov. 9, 2001b.

Shadish, W. R., Newman, D. L., Scheirer, M. A., and Wye, C. (eds.). *Guiding Principles for Evaluators.* New Directions for Program Evaluation, no. 66. San Francisco: Jossey-Bass, 1995.

Silver, J. "The Mechanics of Mainstreaming." Paper presented during session 521 at the annual meeting of the American Evaluation Association, St. Louis, Nov. 9, 2001.

Stake, R. E. *The Art of Case Research.* Thousand Oaks, Calif.: Sage, 1995.

Stake, R. E. "Costs and Benefits of Mainstreaming Evaluation." Paper presented during session 700 at the annual meeting of the American Evaluation Association, St. Louis, Nov. 10, 2001.

Stufflebeam, D. L. "The Relevance of the CIPP Evaluation Model for Educational Accountability." *Journal of Research and Development in Education,* 5(1), 1971, 19–25.

Stufflebeam, D. L. "Hazards of Mainstreaming Evaluation Models and a Recommended Remedy." Paper presented during session 700 at the annual meeting of the American Evaluation Association, St. Louis, Nov. 10, 2001a.

Stufflebeam, D. L. "Theories of Action in Program Evaluation." Paper presented during session 569 at the annual meeting of the American Evaluation Association, St. Louis, Nov. 9, 2001b.

Wandersman, A., Flaspohler, P., and Ace, A. "PIE à la mode: Mainstreaming Evaluation in each Program in Every County of a Statewide School Readiness Initiative." Paper presented during session 101 at the annual meeting of the American Evaluation Association, St. Louis, Nov. 7, 2001.

Williams, D. D. "Reflections on Mainstreaming Evaluation." Summary of papers presented during session 790 at the annual meeting of the American Evaluation Association, St. Louis, Nov. 10, 2001.

DAVID D. WILLIAMS is associate professor of instructional psychology and technology in the David O. McKay School of Education at Brigham Young University. He teaches graduate courses in evaluation and research and conducts research on alternative evaluation views and practices.

MARK L. HAWKES is chair of graduate studies in educational technology at Dakota State University. He is also chair of the Distance and Other Educational Technologies AEA Topical Interest Group and former cofounder and cochair of the Theories of Evaluation Topical Interest Group.

INDEX

Back Issue/Subscription Order Form

Copy or detach and send to:
Jossey-Bass, A Wiley Company, 989 Market Street, San Francisco CA 94103-1741

Call or fax toll-free: Phone 888-378-2537 6:30AM – 3PM PST; Fax 888-481-2665

Back Issues: Please send me the following issues at $27 each
(Important: please include series abbreviation and issue number.
For example EV93)

____

____

____

$ __________ Total for single issues

$ __________ SHIPPING CHARGES: SURFACE

	Domestic	Canadian
First Item	$5.00	$6.00
Each Add'l Item	$3.00	$1.50

For next-day and second-day delivery rates, call the number listed above.

Subscriptions Please __start __renew my subscription to *New Directions for Evaluation* for the year 2_____at the following rate:

U.S.	__Individual $80	__Institutional $175
Canada	__Individual $80	__Institutional $215
All Others	__Individual $104	__Institutional $249
Online Subscription		__Institutional $193

For more information about online subscriptions visit www.interscience.wiley.com

$ __________ Total single issues and subscriptions (Add appropriate sales tax for your state for single issue orders. No sales tax for U.S. subscriptions. Canadian residents, add GST for subscriptions and single issues.)

__Payment enclosed (U.S. check or money order only)
__VISA __MC __ AmEx # ____________________ Exp. Date __________

Signature __________________________ Day Phone __________
__ Bill Me (U.S. institutional orders only. Purchase order required.)

Purchase order # ______________________________

Federal Tax ID13559302 **GST 89102 8052**

Name ____________________________________

Address ____________________________________

____

Phone ____________________ E-mail ____________________

For more information about Jossey-Bass, visit our Web site at www.josseybass.com